EMPLOYMENT LAW

CIPD REVISION GUIDE 2005

Alison Bone is Examiner for Employment Law and played a significant role in the development of the latest set of professional standards.

The Chartered Institute of Personnel and Development is the leading publisher of books and reports for personnel and training professionals, students, and all those concerned with the effective management and development of people at work. For details of all our titles, please contact the publishing department:

tel: 020 8263 3387

fax: 020 8263 3850

e-mail: publish@cipd.co.uk

The catalogue of all CIPD titles can be viewed on the CIPD website:

www.cipd.co.uk/bookstore

EMPLOYMENT LAW

CIPD REVISION GUIDE 2005

ALISON BONE

Chartered Institute of Personnel and Development

Published by the Chartered Institute of Personnel and Development,
CIPD House, Camp Road, London SW19 4UX

First published 2005

Design and typesetting by Curran Publishing Services, Norwich
Printed in Great Britain by The Cromwell Press, Trowbridge, Wiltshire

British Library Cataloguing in Publication Data
A catalogue record of this revision guide is available from the
British Library

ISBN 1 84398 099 1

Chartered Institute of Personnel and Development, CIPD House,
Camp Road, London, SW19 4UX
Tel: 020 8971 9000   Fax: 020 8263 3333
Email: cipd@cipd.co.uk   Website: www.cipd.co.uk
Incorporated by Royal Charter. Registered Charity No. 1079797

CONTENTS

List of tables   *vii*
Cases   *viii*
Acknowledgements   *ix*
Preface   *x*

Section I CIPD Professional Standards   **I**
I The CIPD's Employment Law Professional Standards   **3**
Purpose   3
Performance indicators   4
Indicative content   6
Setting the examination   9

Section 2 How to tackle revision and the examination   **15**
2 Revision and examination guidance   **17**
Introduction   17
Carve out the time, but be realistic   17
What's so different about studying law?   18
What materials should I be using?   19
Structuring your notes   20
Learning the sources and citation of authorities   21
Using cases   22
A revision schedule   24

3 Examiner's insights   **26**
Introduction   26
Looking forward to the examination   26
Matters raised in recent examiners' reports   27

Section 3 Examination practice and feedback   **31**
4 Examination questions and feedback   **33**
Section A: the case study   33
Read the question   33
Answer the question   34
Diagnosis: spotting the issues   34
Stating the law and applying it to the facts   36

Structure and commentary   36
Identifying the generic issues   37
Practice papers   40
Section B: short answer questions   59
Section B: questions from previous papers   61

Section 4 Conclusion   **79**
5 Conclusion   **81**

Index   *82*

TABLES

1 Sample flowchart illustrating application of
   TUPE Regulations   65

CASES

Aparou v *Iceland Frozen Foods* [1996] IRLR 119   73
Barber v *Somerset County Council* [2004] IRLR 475   39
BBC v *Hearn* [1977] IRLR 273   64
Bent's Brewery Co Ltd v *Luke Hogan* [1945] 2 All ER 570   64
Burton and Rhule v *De Vere Hotels* [1996] IRLR 596   72
Carmichael v *National Power plc* [2000] IRLR 43   71
Coote v *Granada Hospitality Ltd* [1998] IRLR 656   22, 28
Dacas v *Brook Street Bureau (UK) Ltd* [2004] IRLR 358   22
Dunnachie v *Kingston-upon-Hull Council* [2004] IRLR 287   55
ECM v *Cox* [1999] IRLR 559   65
Egg Stores v *Leibovici* [1976] IRLR 376   78
Ford v *Warwickshire County Council* [1983] IRLR 126   73
Halford v *UK* [1997] IRLR 471   67
Hayward v *Cammell Laird* [1988] IRLR 257   51
ICI v *Shatwell* [1965] AC 656   72
Jones v *Iceland Frozen Foods* [1982] IRLR 439   54
Jones v *Tower Boot* [1997] IRLR 168   48, 72
Johnstone v *Bloomsbury HA* [1991] ICR 269   73
Kwik-Fit v *Lineham* [1992] IRLR 156   47
Lister v *Hesley Hall Ltd* [2001] 2 All ER 769   72
Macdonald and Pearce [2003] IRLR 512   78
Marshalls Clay Products v *Caulfield* [2003] IRLR 552   75
Oy Liikenne [2001] IRLR 171   65
Pepper v *Webb* [1969] 2 All ER 216   23
Polkey v *AE Dayton Services* [1987] IRLR 13   23, 54
Reed and Bull v *Stedman* [1999] IRLR 299   48
Robertson v *Preston CC* (unreported)   75
Rookes v *Barnard* [1964] AC 1129 HL   64
Safeway Stores plc v *Burrell* [1997] IRLR 200   69
Scala Ballroom (Wolverhampton) Ltd v *Ratcliffe* [1958] 3 All ER 220   64
Shields v *E Coomes (Holdings) Ltd* [1978] ICR 1159   51
Sophie Redmond Stichting v *Bartol and others* [1992] IRLR 366   64
Spijkers v *Gebroeders Benedik Abattoir CV* [1986] ECR 1119   64, 65
Spring v *Guardian Assurance plc [1994] IRLR 460*   28
Süzen v *Zehnacker* [1997] IRLR 255   65
Timeplan Education Group Ltd v *National Union of Teachers*
    [1997] IRLR 457   63
Western Excavating v *Sharp* [1978] IRLR 27   47, 69
Williams v *Compair Maxam Ltd* [1982] IRLR 83   70

ACKNOWLEDGEMENTS

As always, thanks to the support teams – Anthony, Alex, Imogen and Erica at home, the law group at the University of Brighton especially James, Judith and Lucy who picked up pieces I didn't mean to drop and the others who were just there when needed – you know who you are.

Alison Bone
CIPD Examiner in Employment Law
July 2004

PREFACE

The writing of the first edition of this study guide was started in May 2003 as the first students to sit the new CIPD Professional Development Standard (PDS) Employment Law examination were doing their final revision and preparation. They were the pioneers and did not have a revision guide to help them, although their tutors would have given them plenty of advice and support. There is much material in this guide that is generic in that it will apply to all law examinations taken by all students at all times, but it still needs to be stated. One of my tasks as the CIPD examiner is to visit centres and talk to students about how best to prepare for the examination. Much of what I write merely reinforces what tutors have been saying throughout the course, although many people tell me that students take a little more notice because it is I who say it. My first piece of advice is therefore to listen carefully to what your tutors tell you: they have a wealth of experience in teaching, and many of them will have taken CIPD or other law examinations themselves and therefore know what is required. This guide focuses on the examination, since the assignment, which all CIPD students must take and pass, varies in form from centre to centre and is internally marked before being externally moderated.

This second edition is published after three cohorts of students have sat the 'new' examination. Indeed the old examination is being phased out at the end of 2004, so I do not intend to compare the 'old' and 'new' formats. I am also aware that employment law is unique in that for all other subjects, students are aiming for a CIPD qualification and studying other subjects at the same time and probably reading other revision guides, whereas those studying for an Advanced Certificate in Employment Law are only doing this one examination, and many of them are already CIPD qualified. If you fall into the former category there is much generic material on revision technique contained in Chapter 2 that you might wish to skim through, although I have tried to give it a law bias.

Since the first edition I have had the benefit of (anonymous) feedback from a number of reviewers. My thanks to them for their largely constructive comments, many of which I have acted on.

There were some comments that were diametrically opposed, for example, 'I would like to see more on subject content' was countered by 'it is not necessary to list subject content' – which simply illustrates that you can't please all of the people any of the time. I was also told my writing style sometimes comes across as slightly patronising, but I'm afraid that I've written so many books in the same way I don't think I could change now. I hope the legal parts are sufficiently dour!

I have taken many examinations in my time. As a legal academic I became interested early in my career in the assessment process, and decided that I could only empathise fully with my students if I kept putting myself through the ordeal of assessment. As a result I have amassed five 'A' levels (the latest, in French, obtained in 1996) in addition to various degrees, certificates and diplomas. I do not like examinations as an assessment mechanism, but I am now getting quite good at them, having had plenty of practice. I have also set and marked over 200 examinations, and this has given me an insight into the process. It is a delicious irony that although students can learn how to pass examinations, many examiners are never taught how to set them, but this guide will help you 'get inside my head' and see what it is that you need to write in order to earn those valuable marks which will get you through.

The guide is broken down into four sections. The first (Chapter 1) deals with the CIPD Professional Standards, and gives a summary of key content and how this is reflected in the types of questions set, with examples and guidance for revision. The second section (Chapters 2 and 3) provides general techniques for revising employment law, including time management, the need for wider reading, and developing analytical and problem-solving skills. The most recent examination (May 2004) is used as the focus for examiner feedback in Chapter 3, with examples from student scripts. Section 3 – the largest section – consists of Chapter 4 which concentrates on the three PDS Employment Law papers that have been set to date: May 2003, November 2003 and May 2004, and gives pointers as to how the marks were allocated in terms of style and content, with examples from both the good and some of the weaker scripts. Because some of the topics are already showing their age (employment law moves so quickly!) not all questions are given equal weighting in terms of coverage. Section 4 provides a brief conclusion.

This book is aimed mainly at those sitting the nationally assessed examination, but the guidance on answering questions is intended to be transferable and so should be of assistance for those studying internally assessed employment law courses. It is important to note that the book is only intended as a supplement to the main course textbooks.

Employment law is an essential subject for personnel practitioners, and a recent qualification in the subject will give you the edge if you are job-hunting or seeking promotion. It is unfortunate that it keeps changing all the time, but it is this tendency that makes it such a valuable commodity.

I wish you good luck with your studies.

Alison Bone
CIPD examiner in Employment Law

SECTION 1

CIPD PROFESSIONAL STANDARDS

1 THE CIPD'S EMPLOYMENT LAW PROFESSIONAL STANDARDS

The following is based on the standards issued by the CIPD for the Professional Standard Employment Law.

Purpose

The volume of employment law has increased rapidly because of national legislation, the social dimension of the European Union, and case law based on interpretation of both national legislation and European decisions. Many areas that were considered relatively straightforward have become increasingly complex and more detailed. Personnel professionals need to advise other managers on existing law.

However, professional personnel and development practitioners need to take employment law beyond mere compliance. To add real value they should be capable of anticipating and evaluating proposed changes in the law, so that the organisation can plan, prepare and implement sound personnel policies. Personnel professionals must also be able to advise management about the implications of existing and impending legislation on resources and business objectives.

Personnel professionals who meet this Standard will be able to ensure their organisation retains its competitive advantage by not falling foul of the law. In the event of legal action by an employee, the personnel professional will be a valuable resource who can:

- take instructions quickly
- analyse the situation effectively
- represent the company at an employment tribunal, if necessary.

Performance indicators

The full Standards include operational and knowledge performance indicators. These are both given in full here.

Operational indicators

These 11 performance indicators are all examples of how it is possible to demonstrate competence by actions other than by writing, although sometimes writing may form part of the action: for example, in preparing a witness statement. Given this is a specialist standard you may not have the opportunity to practise all of these at work, but you should be aware of the activities, and good assignments will require you to demonstrate many of these skills, as they will be stated clearly in the assessment criteria.

Practitioners must be able to:

1. Work with, and find their way through, legal materials, including precedents, case law and legislation.

2. Analyse legal materials capably and confidently.

3. Act as the primary adviser to the organisation on employment law, and thus make a contribution that helps prevent the organisation falling foul of relevant legislation or regulations.

4. Read and explain an Act of Parliament and a European directive.

5. Use appropriate sources of information and find the information needed to keep up to date with case law and so on.

6. Represent their organisation in employment tribunal proceedings, or instruct/brief a solicitor if or when appropriate.

7. Prepare the organisation's witnesses who are to give evidence at an employment tribunal.

8. Give advice on the stages at which the content of proposed legislation can be influenced by an organisation.

9. Explain the law – actual and intended – in language and concepts that non-legal management colleagues understand and can absorb.

10. Implement relevant and appropriate practice in:

- recruitment
- employment and contracts
- termination of employment
- employee relations policies
- procedures based on legal principles and codes of practice.

11. Advise on and evaluate the likely impact of actual and intended legislation on the organisation's policies, practices and resources.

Knowledge indicators

These eight knowledge indicators can be measured by writing and may be assessed in the examination. Any employment law textbook will cover all of these topics, but it is very important to ensure the book is up to date: for example, the CIPD book *Essentials of employment law* by David Lewis and Malcolm Sergeant (8th edition) was published in February 2004.

The indicators are not to be treated as examination 'topics' as is the case with many others of the CIPD Professional Standards, where it is possible to link the indicators to particular chapters of a book. Employment law is a holistic subject and some of the indicators below can only be understood in the context of another, for example, the role of the Central Arbitration Committee is clearly linked with the legal principles associated with collective employment. The indicative content (see below) gives a clearer breakdown of separate study areas.

Practitioners must understand and be able to explain:

1. The legal principles associated with the employment of people, both individually and collectively.

2. The influence of European Union employment law, particularly the impact of EU directives and the way they are transposed into national legislation.

3. The role of employment law in delivering the organisation's business objectives.

4. The role of the Central Arbitration Committee (CAC) in determining claims for statutory trade union recognition and de-recognition.

5. The influence of ACAS in resolving individual and collective employment disputes.

6. How individual employee employment law enshrines good (best fit) personnel practices.

7. New developments in legislation and case law in both the UK and EU, and their impact potential on an organisation's policies and practices.

8. The benefit to the organisation of having a personnel and development practitioner with expertise in the relevant laws and regulations.

Indicative content

The following is a direct quote from the standards. The content covers everything that will be covered by your studies although more emphasis will be put on some aspects than others as is explained below.

The institutions of employment law

*   The civil and criminal court structure
*   Employment and employment appeal tribunals; the labour court system
*   The Central Arbitration Committee (CAC), Advisory Conciliation and Arbitration Service (ACAS), Health and Safety Commission (HSC), Commission for Racial Equality (CRE)
*   The European Court of Justice, the Court of Human Rights.

Individual employment law

*   The nature and terms of the employment contract, the impact of employment protection legislation and:

  - maternity rights
  - time-off provisions, including parental leave and caring for dependants
  - holidays
  - working time
  - pay and deductions.
- The law relating to:
  - advertising
  - interviewing
  - fixed-term contracts
  - temporary, part-time and casual employment
  - use of probationary periods
  - use of union and non-union labour.
- Legislation and case law covering:
  - race, gender and disability discrimination
  - dignity at work (harassment, bullying, whistleblowing)
  - equal pay
  - privacy
  - human rights.
- Termination of employment and:
  - the concept of breach of contract
  - legislation and case law relating to unfair dismissal
  - redundancy procedures and payments
  - the Transfer of Undertakings Regulations.
- Individual employee rights to be represented by a trade union (Employment Relations Act 1999).

Collective employment law

- The law relating to:
  - collective bargaining and agreements
  - freedom of association
  - disclosure of information
  - time off for trade union duties
  - statutory trade union recognition and de-recognition.
- The law relating to industrial conflict and:
  - the boundaries of lawful action
  - damages for unlawful action
  - the labour injunction; picketing
  - dismissal in industrial disputes.
- Transnational information and consultation.

Confidential information and intellectual property

- Patents, inventions and copyright.
- Protection of confidential information and the:
  - Data Protection Act
  - Access to Medical Reports Act
  - Access to Health Records Act
  - references.

Health and safety at work

- The legal framework and:
  - safety representatives and committees
  - safety policies
  - enforcement of health and safety legislation

    –   the rights and obligations of individual employees.
- Rights and duties of employers and employees in relation to:
    –   injuries at work
    –   negligence
    –   breach of statutory duty
    –   working time
    –   stress.

The indicative content is only intended as a guide to the topics that comprise the CIPD Employment Law elective and were not written by the examiner. It is already showing its age, since the Employment Act 2002 has added to the list of rights and duties of employers and employees, and the EU Employment Framework Directive has meant that discrimination law has been expanded to cover sexual orientation, religion or belief, and will soon cover age. Most tutors are aware that trying to define the boundaries of a subject such as employment law is like painting the Forth Bridge, and will make students aware that current developments are fair game for the examination even though they may not be specifically listed.

Setting the examination

The May and November examinations are normally drafted around the end of the previous year, and the November examination is revisited in July to make any necessary modifications. The examination tends to be topical and to highlight issues that personnel practitioners have to get to grips with either in the recent past or in the near future. If a case is reported in the newspaper on the day of the examination or a new law was passed a few days before, marks will be awarded if it is mentioned where relevant, even though of course it may not have been known about at the time the question was set.

The institutions of employment law

As will be explained later, although it is necessary to be familiar with the roles of, for instance, employment tribunals and the various commissions overseeing discrimination law and policy, they would not be the subjects of a specific question, but their work may need to be referred to when answering a question on an associated topic.

Individual employment law

This enormous topic is subdivided in the indicative content into sub-topics that do not match easily the approach taken by the authors of the textbooks. Individual employment law is perhaps more easily broken down as follows.

The nature and form of the working relationship

The main working relationship used to be that of employer and employee and most rights attached to this, but recently new legislative rights have tended to be extended to 'workers'. This definition and which rights workers and other 'non-employees' possess is important. The tests used by the courts to establish employee status such as the control, organisation and multiple approach are included, as is the approach taken by the courts to dealing with casual workers, agency workers, temporary and part-time workers and those on fixed-term contracts. Other minor aspects of this topic such as office holders, directors, Crown employees, those on a probationary period, children and foreign employees may be referred to tangentially, but would not normally justify a whole question.

The formation and content of the contract of employment

This is a very rich source of material and there are several areas that need to be addressed including:

• Sources of the contract of employment: express terms, implied terms, collective agreements, works rules and staff handbooks, custom and practice and statute, some of which are addressed in more detail below and in other sections. The provisions of s1 Employment Rights Act (ERA) 1996 need to be understood, as do remedies available if a written statement is not provided. Minimum statutory notice periods are covered (s86(1) ERA) as are the new statutory provisions covering discipline and grievance procedures.

- Implied terms cover a wide range of aspects such as the duty of the employee to obey reasonable orders and the employer to pay wages, if not provide work. This extends to the effect of sickness and lay-off. The duty of fidelity of employees and former employees is affected by the law on restraint of trade including restrictive covenants, their legality and enforcement, and garden leave. The ever-expanding duty of implied trust and confidence is relevant to the discussion of breach of contract and constructive dismissal.

- The law relating to references: defamation, negligence and discrimination.

- Variation of contract: when and how variation can be achieved and the legal sanctions if agreement is not reached.

Discrimination in employment

This is another enormous area of law, which as stated above continues to expand. It includes:

- The different types of discrimination including those currently covered by UK law and those proposed by EU legislation: sex, race, disability, sexual orientation, religion or belief, age, those with criminal records, trade union members and non-members.

- Forms of discrimination: direct, indirect and victimisation, with examples including discrimination in recruitment, promotion, terms during contract including dress codes and mobility, liability for contract workers.

- All forms of harassment.

- Pregnancy and discrimination.

- Permissible discrimination, positive action and genuine occupational requirement.

- Vicarious liability and defences.

- Disability definition, examples from cases and the code of practice, justification, reasonable adjustments.

- Bringing a claim, the questionnaire procedure, burden of proof and remedies.

- Equal pay: like work, work rated as equivalent, work of equal value. Defences available. Use of equal pay questionnaires.

Individual employment rights

This topic includes:

- Maternity, paternity, adoption and parental rights including time off work for ante-natal care; risk assessment and suspension on maternity grounds; ordinary and additional maternity leave; maternity pay and allowance; parental leave and flexible working.

- Guaranteed payments; suspension on medical grounds; time off work for public duties, to look for work and to care for dependants; rights of employee representatives, jury service and other time off; Sunday trading; access to medical reports, statutory sick pay.

- Working Time Regulations: hours, rest periods, holiday, derogations.

- Wages: when and how lawful deductions can be made; remedies for wrongful deductions.

- The right to privacy: European Convention provisions and Human Rights Act; Regulation of Investigatory Powers Act; Data Protection Act and control of computer and personal data.

Termination of employment

This includes:

- Disciplinary, dismissal and grievance procedures including statutory dispute resolution procedures; the right to be accompanied.

- Continuity of employment.

- Termination by notice, notice periods, breach of contract and wrongful dismissal.

- Termination as a result of frustration.

- Unfair dismissal: eligibility to claim, written reasons for dismissal, reasons for dismissal, automatically unfair reasons, reasonable procedure, remedies.

- Redundancy: statutory definition, renewal or re-engagement, offer of suitable alternative employment, unfair selection, redundancy payments calculations.

- Dismissals in connection with transfers of undertakings and industrial action and the protection afforded in relation to whistleblowing.

Collective employment law

- An outline knowledge of the law relating to trade unions including rights of members and officials, disciplinary action and breach of union rules.

- Voluntary and statutory recognition procedures: collective bargaining and the disclosure of information.

- Transnational information and consultation: the Directive and its implementation.

- Legal liabilities of trade unions including the economic torts; the 'golden formula' statutory protection and loss of immunities; damages and injunctions.

- The law of industrial conflict: picketing and the Code of Practice; criminal and civil liability.

Health and safety at work

- Criminal liability under the Health and Safety at Work Act 1974.

- The development of European law and its impact.

- Liability of the employer in negligence for the health and safety of employees and visitors; safe system of work, premises, plant, and fellow workers; stress and psychiatric illness; vicarious liability.

SECTION 2

HOW TO TACKLE REVISION
AND THE EXAMINATION

2 REVISION AND EXAMINATION GUIDANCE

Introduction

For many of you Employment Law is just one of a series of examinations that must be passed before you can become a member of the CIPD. For a few of you, perhaps doing an Advanced Certificate in Employment Law or similar course, the only examination you will be taking is that in Employment Law. Whatever your situation, the tactics to be adopted need to be a little different from other subject study patterns. Before I discuss the differences, here is a short reminder of the basics, which apply whatever you are studying.

Carve out the time, but be realistic

Studying and revising is rather like going on a diet. We pretend that we are going to change the habits of a lifetime but most of us see it as a means to an end, a quick fix so that we can revert as soon as practically possible to our 'normal' life. But quick fixes don't work! You do need to change life patterns for months and months, and if you are serious about keeping up to date with employment law because your job demands it, this really will need to become a weekly, if not a daily duty.

In order to study and revise effectively you will need to juggle the other demands on your time and make devoted space for this activity. A few of you – the lucky ones – will be in total control of your time, in that you will have a free choice how to spend out-of-work hours, but for most the social demands of others such as partners, children, friends and parents, plus the necessities of life including feeding, washing and cleaning yourself, dependants, clothes, house and dog, mean that some planning will be essential. It is important to be realistic. If we go back to the dieting analogy, of course it is possible to lose 10 kilograms of weight in a month, but you have to be the size of a sumo wrestler at the beginning and do nothing but sit quietly, eating fruit and vegetables and the odd piece of fish. And the weight you lose will mainly be because of muscle wastage and fluid loss. So don't pretend you are going to spend every Saturday and every other weekday evening studying, but do plan your spare time to accommodate your study. How many hours should you spend every week? Like dieting, it is impossible to say how long it will take, as so much depends on personal factors. There will be some days – or more likely evenings –after a hard day at work, when even opening a book will seem a waste of time, whereas on other days, when the competing duty is walking the dog and it's pouring with rain, curling up with the 'Law at work' section in *People Management* might seem positively attractive. Some of you will be able to benefit from odd snatches of study time, 30 minutes here, an hour there, whereas the majority will want to dedicate a big chunk of time, knowing they need time to settle into study mode before becoming productive.

What's so different about studying law?

As stated in the Preface, there is much advice here that is generic and will apply whatever subject is being studied. Although as the examiner I do not teach CIPD students, I do teach employment law to undergraduate and postgraduate students who are studying other courses too, and their feedback every year indicates that they need to spend far more time reading the materials for employment law than for the other subjects they study. Some aspects of the law are difficult to absorb and need time to digest, but it is not just the difficult bits that demand the time. As one law student said: 'you can't waffle in law and there is not much that is just obvious common sense – in fact some of the cases clearly contradict each other and are confusing'. It is a good lesson to learn and the mark of a perceptive student that law can be confusing. If it never appears to be so, then the tutor has cut out all the tricky bits and you are not doing enough reading of the set texts!

Employment law is not really a series of separate topics but one large topic, which has to be divided up for teaching and learning purposes. It is a very useful exercise to draw a mind map[1] as your study progresses, slotting in the different topics and links between them. Sharing these with others and discussing similarities and differences is also a stimulating revision aid. Different topics such as 'recruitment' or 'redundancy' can similarly be mind-mapped, and refined versions are very useful as revision material.

What materials should I be using?

The CIPD publish a list of books[2] that are recommended for student use, but there are around 30 textbooks on employment law currently in print, all of which have something to recommend them. Distance flexible learning courses will have their own bespoke material, which is usually updated annually. The CIPD list is also updated annually, but publication of employment law books tend to coincide with recent developments rather than match the start of the academic year. The most important quality of any book is that it is the latest edition available: with the passing of the Employment Act 2002 any book published prior to 2002 is likely to be out of date. Because of the wide choice available it is best practice to take the lead from your tutor. Often the choice is made partly on what has proved best in former students' experience, and tutors understand there is no point choosing a book that they think is readable and user-friendly if the students vote otherwise and buy and read something else.

The employment law examination is the only one of the CIPD examinations in which it is allowable to take in materials. An unmarked copy of a statute book is permitted, and ideally you will be using this throughout your course to familiarise yourself with the contents and the layout. It is common practice for students on other law courses to take a statute book into the examination. Students with experience of this make it clear that it is really only an emotional crutch as there is very little time to look things up. High-lighting of relevant passages is permitted but no other marks must be made on the text. Blank sticky notes (different colours are useful) can be used to bookmark important pages.

Apart from reading a textbook and a statute book you should be keeping up to date by accessing other legal sources. The law pages in *People Management* have already been mentioned, and there are also useful articles in *Personnel Today*. More academic discussions including research findings of the impact of the law on organisations can be found in the *Industrial Law Journal*. There are many other legal journals, such as *IDS Brief*, to which, if you are working, your organisation may subscribe, but the most important legal developments are usually highlighted in the national broadsheet newspapers and on radio programmes such as *Today* on BBC Radio 4. The Business sections in Sunday newspapers also often have useful articles, and of course there are an enormous number of websites, including that of the CIPD, which have links to summaries of material.[3] Finally, there are many websites that provide legal updates and material including those of the CIPD (www.cipd.co.uk), *People Management*, *Personnel Today* (www.personneltoday.com) and the barrister Daniel Barnett (www.danielbarnett.co.uk). Government websites such as www.dti.gov.uk are useful in giving commencement dates and summaries of complex legislation.

Don't forget that your own organisation may also prove to be a useful resource if it is a large one. If you work with people who have recently studied employment law or who have responsibility for giving legal advice, ask if you can sit in on meetings where legal issues are to be discussed. Students who have some practical context in which to configure their study of employment law find it much easier to understand.

Structuring your notes

There is no right order or way to learn employment law – as stated above, it is really one great big topic. Some courses start with the institutions: the role of ACAS and the CAC, for example; others with where the law comes from or, because this has been covered previously, the different types of relationship between employer and worker. However your course is organised, you need to ensure that once a topic has been concluded your notes are in a format from which you can revise. This means that you have followed up any queries you have about the material and done any necessary supplementary reading, which of course may raise other issues. Ideally, your course will enable you to discuss issues with others and a tutor, and provide opportunities to practise answering questions that could be set in the examination. The new PDS emphasises the importance of research, and there will be at least two questions on each paper in Section B (and more in the future) that specifically require you to give evidence that you have read about recent research. 'Research' can be interpreted liberally to mean contextual comment or perhaps an author's view on the significance of a recent case, but there must be more than a mere statement of the relevant law or the answer will score a fail mark. Examples are discussed later in the book in Chapter 4.

Many of the other issues dealt with in this chapter are to do with how to answer employment law examination questions, but need to be taken into account when getting your notes into order for revision purposes.

Learning the sources and citation of authorities

The purpose of the examination is to assess whether you are familiar with the key employment law issues as set out in the standards. There is not much law that could be labelled 'common sense' – in fact one of the complaints small businesses are always raising is that there is so much law, and it is so complex and bureaucratic, that they are unable to keep pace with it. If you do give the 'right' guidance (more below about what is meant by 'right') you will score very few marks unless you quote the relevant source.

Here's an example:

> Employers must give details of main terms of employment within eight weeks.

There is nothing wrong with this sentence, but the following is more accurate, gives more information, and states the source, using the phrase in the relevant statute and, given of course the context of the question, is likely to score a higher mark:

> Employers are obliged by s1 of the Employment Rights Act 1996 to give all employees a written statement of particulars which sets out the main terms of their contract within eight weeks of the start of employment.

This particular example quotes the section number because it happens to be section 1, with which your examiner is familiar, but it is unrealistic to expect you (or any personnel professional) to be familiar with all section numbers of all the statutes, and there is no point in wasting valuable time in the examination looking them up. This guide does give all the section numbers where appropriate, but of course it is not being written under examination conditions and is meant to be a source of reference. The relevant statute name and year must be stated accurately (there is *no* excuse for 'Racial Discrimination Act', as has appeared in the past). It is perfectly permissible to use an abbreviation if a statute is quoted more than once, but it should be stated in full on the first occasion, for example:

> The Sex Discrimination Act 1975 (SDA) covers both gender and marital discrimination. Any claims under the SDA must normally be made within three months of the act that forms the basis of the complaint.

Using cases

One of the questions tutors are often asked is how many cases have to be learned and how much detail needs to be reproduced. Cases in employment law are of two types, the first being those that really change the direction of the law, such as *Coote* v *Granada Hospitality Ltd*[4] (a case which established an employer could be liable for post-employment discrimination) while the second type are examples of ongoing developments, such as *Dacas* v *Brook Street Bureau (UK) Ltd* [5] (a case concerning the status of agency workers). There are fewer cases that fall into the first category, and it is important that you try to commit some of them to memory. It is impossible to tell you how many should be learned, but your tutor will stress certain cases and make it clear that they are fundamental.

I sometimes use the analogy of learning to speak a foreign language. It is possible to communicate without using verbs, but people will understand you better if you can use a few. Cases similarly aid the communication of the principles that permeate employment law, and quoting them demonstrates not only that you have learned them but also that through your choice, you understand the relevant principle. In some areas of the law, such as breach of contract, the duty of implied trust and confidence being an obvious example, the law can only be stated accurately by looking at case examples, simply because there is no relevant statute.

Of course you cannot earn marks in an examination just for quoting cases – they have to be relevant to the question!

A good examination script will ideally contain a selection of cases that illustrate key points, and where appropriate demonstrate an understanding of recent developments in the law. It is possible to obtain a distinction without quoting many cases, but generally speaking a script without cases tends to score fewer marks. For very recent cases, that is, within 18 months of the examination, the year is useful and generally easy to remember, but the year is usually not required to be quoted for other cases. Accurate reproduction of the parties' names, however, is important. There are a few cases that even lawyers tend to refer to by the name of the applicant, the classic example being *Polkey*, [6] but good academic practice is to produce the names of both parties in full. In coursework you will be expected to give the full case citation, ie year, report and page number, but in the examination the names alone are sufficient. Of course, if you forget the names of one of the parties you must just quote the one that you recall but do not be tempted to write 'this is illustrated by the case of _____ v _____', hoping that the names will suddenly emerge in a blinding flash later. They usually will not, but if you do recall a case that you wish to quote you can always add a footnote at the bottom of the page, annotated appropriately.

If you really cannot remember the case name at all, as a last resort you could give a few key facts, but remember the importance of case law is the reason that the judge reached the decision he or she did, not the facts that led to the case being heard. As an example, suppose you are setting out the duties of an employee in an examination answer and have forgotten entirely the parties' names in *Pepper* v *Webb*.[7] The summary:

> In one case a gardener who swore at the wife of his employer and refused to carry out instructions was held to have been in breach of contract, not by swearing but by refusing to obey reasonable orders

will score a few marks. On the other hand, this might not score any:

> There was a case where a gardener said he didn't care about the 'sodding garden' and was sacked and this was held to be breach of contract by him.

In certain instances there may be no reason for giving the facts of the case at all, especially where there has been a run of cases on a particular issue, for instance, whether an agency worker is an employee of the client company. It would thus be acceptable to state:

> Mutuality of obligation between the agency worker and the client company may indicate an employer/employee relationship, as in *Dacas* v *Brook Street Bureau (UK) Ltd*

and this would earn marks.

A revision schedule

It will not be a surprise to learn that the topic you covered first in the course is likely to be the one you start revising first, and thus the one you tend to know best by the time you come to the examination. Unfortunately, the reverse is true for the topics at the end of the course: they might be covered in less detail by the tutor if there are time pressures, and might be revised selectively by you if you feel you have covered enough topics to give you a reasonable choice in the examination. The examination structure is dealt with in detail later, but it is never wise to limit your choices too much. The examination covers many topics but there are often subtopics within them, and sometimes questions are relatively focused. It follows that a question requiring you to discuss consultation in relation to collective redundancies and transfers of undertakings will not need a general statement setting out, for example, the definition of redundancy, and answers giving case law on how courts have interpreted the definition will also not earn marks.

My best examination result ever was 'A' level law, which I sat many, many years ago after teaching it at evening class as part of my first lecturing post. My students discovered early on that although I had a law degree I had never sat 'A' level law, and said that I should take it too. I became a detective. I pored over past examination papers, I read avidly all the examiner reports, and I came up with a list of topics that almost always came up in one form or another. Then I drew up a list of less popular topics that occasionally came up. Finally, there was a list of what I labelled 'awkward' aspects of popular topics. I gave these to my students, and we practised drawing up draft answers: which points needed to be made, which statutes and cases would be quoted, and good introductions and conclusions that pulled together the main threads. Almost all the class passed the examination, and I acquired a grade A. It is the only examination I have ever sat where I knew what was required for each answer to each question. This is the secret of all examination success: knowing what the question requires you to do, and then doing it.

Your revision schedule should include looking at past papers as an indicator of likely topics and approaches. Although the PDS Employment Law examination papers reflect new CIPD standards, there is much to be gained by looking at former PQS papers and their related examiners' reports, since general examination technique is discussed there too. Practising examination technique is essential. If your course has a 'mock' examination, make sure you take it and learn from the feedback. If your course does not have one, request that one is included! Some tutors complain that there is barely enough time to cover the syllabus as it is, but of course it is possible to do examinations on your own at home under suitable conditions – it is knowing how fast you can think and write under pressure that provides the learning experience, plus of course the feedback on what was required.

Notes

1. An excellent aid to any study: guidance on how to do it can be found at www.mind-map.com/mindmaps_howto.htm
2. http://www.cipd.co.uk/download/registered/06_RecommendedReadingListForCandidates.pdf
3. http://www.cipd.co.uk/EmploymentLaw/Home/Default.htm
4. [1998] IRLR 656.
5. [2004] IRLR 358.
6. *Polkey* v *AE Dayton Services* [1987] IRLR 13.
7. [1969] 2 All ER 216.

3 EXAMINER'S INSIGHTS

Introduction

This chapter looks at general issues raised in previous examiners' reports (including those relating to the examinations in November 2003 and May 2004) but transcribes them into advice for those of you taking the examination in the future. It is a short chapter because the generic advice is almost always the same for all ((employment) law) examinations. The sad truth is that every time a new batch of students takes the examination, a number repeat the same mistakes made by students who preceded them.

As stated in the previous chapter it is therefore very important to read the examiners' reports, not just to discover what particular aspects of law were being tested, and what the general good and bad points were in relation to content, but to get tips on style and how to ensure what is written earns as many marks as possible.

Looking forward to the examination

Of course nobody relishes the prospect of an examination, but this section gives a quick overview on style and other aspects of presentation that may help earn a few marks and which can be encouraged by good study practices.

- Ensure your spelling is of reasonable standard, especially legal words. Some tutors dictate notes, and it is possible that you may be uncertain of some spellings. Any errors should be picked up by reading the recommended text. Reading about time off for 'anti-natal care' may be slightly amusing for the marker but at a deeper level it reflects either ignorance or carelessness or both.

- Writing styles should be clear and concise. Although bullet points are permissible, they should, as in this guide, be supported by sufficient detail. Only if you are really pushed for time should bullet points consist of lists of words. In an emergency a few words might earn a mark or two, but never, ever, write 'sorry, out of time' on any examination script. It only indicates poor time management.

- Bad grammar, like spelling, detracts from the quality of your script. Dyslexic students will normally have received extra guidance and sometimes time to check their work, and the standard of their work is usually good. I have certain pet hates: the misuse of the apostrophe, especially in 'its' and 'it's', and the confusion of the verbs and noun 'affect' and 'effect'. Of course, I will not fail a paper just because of poor grammar and spelling, but if the overall mark is just below the pass borderline I might not be able to award an extra mark or two for clear presentation. This may cause controversy – but it is honest and explicit.

- Practise writing under time constraints and check your legibility. It is only under examination conditions that most of you will ever be called upon to write quickly, and undoubtedly we will all be using word processors in a few years' time, but occasionally scripts are very difficult to translate. Given the short time in which examiners have to turn round the scripts, it is not feasible to ask others to have a go at working out what some scribbles are attempting to communicate.

- Follow the guidelines in the answer books. Examiners need the margins to write marks and comments, so if you forget something, make a clear mark such as an asterisk and insert the additional material at the end of the answer, or, if necessary, the end of the script. Ideally, each section of the case study and each Section B answer should commence on a new page to leave space for later additions.

- Make your cases and statute names stand out. You will want to do this in your notes, and it is a practice that should be carried over in the examination room. Different coloured pens may be too time-consuming but underlining or writing case names in capitals may be an alternative.

Matters raised in recent examiners' reports

Below is a collection of points raised in recent examiners' reports.

- Given there is a choice of topics in Section B it is important to revise a sufficient number of topics in depth. Weak students may well attempt all seven questions but is often clear that their knowledge on the last one or two topics is very limited. (May and November 2003, May 2004)

- Following on from the above, it is important that the answer does not just address the general topic area but answers the question set. This is the main reason why students fail and is repeated at many points throughout this book. As an example, in May 2003 there was the Section B question:

> In what circumstances (if any) may it be more dangerous to refuse to give a reference than to provide one?

Some answers were able to set out the general law on references clearly and to discuss the need to be accurate and objective to avoid negligence liability (*Spring* v *Guardian Assurance plc*)[1], thus answering the second part of the question about the dangers of providing a reference. It was comparatively rare however for an answer to address clearly the first part of the question, that is, the dangers of refusing to provide a reference, which require a discussion of victimisation as an aspect of discrimination as illustrated by *Coote* v *Granada Hospitality Ltd.*[2] Those of you who are really astute will notice that the answer requires extra detail – the word 'more' requires some comparison of the 'danger' of being liable in discrimination as opposed to negligence, which invites a brief discussion of the remedies available for successful applicants. Virtually nobody picked up this subtlety, but it is a lot to ask in an answer that has to be written in a few minutes. Such an answer would earn a mark in the 70s or 80s, that is, a distinction, assuming the other points had also been addressed.

To get back to the original point, a general answer covering the law of references would be unlikely to score a pass mark.

It seems rather obvious but one way to ensure your answer does address the question set is to incorporate it into your opening sentence, for example:

It may be more dangerous to refuse to give a reference than provide one because an employer could be held liable for victimisation, a form of discrimination which is addressed by all the statutes i.e., the Sex Discrimination Act 1975, the Race Relations Act 1976 and the Disability Discrimination Act 1995 …

- A general absence of Master's-level ('M'-level) thinking. Many of the questions in Section B (but not necessarily all) will require a demonstration of critical or analytical thought – as illustrated by the 'reference' question example above. Answers that require such analysis will usually fail if the answer is just generally descriptive. Other subjects covered by the CIPD standards draw heavily on the BACKUP framework, which highlights five competencies:

  - business orientation

  - application capability

  - knowledge of the subject matter

  - understanding

  - persuasion and presentation skills.

  These do not all translate very easily into a legal context, which is why I prefer to emphasise the requirement of 'M'-level/ 'post-graduateness' of the answers. Sometimes this can be evidenced by showing an understanding of the context in which the law has developed, which in turn will be illustrated by evidence of wider reading. This is crucial when the question requires you to refer to recent research (see Chapter 2), because an answer that ignores such an instruction will almost always fail. This was noted in both November 2003 and May 2004 examiners' reports.

- Answers must quote the law applicable at the time the examination is set. Almost all employment law claims have to be brought within three months of the act which is the subject of the complaint, and applicants cannot therefore hang about waiting for the law to change in their favour! In the November 2003 paper the Section A case study involved a small business employing 12 employees. The Disability Discrimination Act 1995 was therefore inapplicable because of the existing small business exemption but a large number of candidates made statements such as: 'It would be different if this scenario occurred after October 2004' and then went on to answer the question in the future as if in a *Dr Who* time warp. One even wrote: 'I will assume for the purposes of this answer that this business is covered by the DDA', thus implying that the examinee knew it was not, but was going to ignore that crucial point.

* Be precise. Vague statements that contain no law but give general warnings that there could be legal implications for certain action (or lack of action) do not earn marks. An example was given in the November 2003 report on a question involving the implications of the (then) impending Religion or Belief and Sexual Orientation Regulations where one student wrote:

> It is important to be vigilant and careful.

This did not score any marks.

A general framework for a Section A case study answer, which is adopted by many tutors throughout the country, is to state the relevant law clearly and apply it to the problem. To this should be added (as stated in the May 2004 report) that 'relevant law' should include any available defences, and the appropriate remedies should also be discussed. The Section A case study in May 2004 involved a potential equal pay claim by a woman. Some said that if it were established that she had a good claim (and details were given of the various possibilities under the Equal Pay Act 1970) then 'the employer should make up the difference'. This meant that the allocation of marks for setting out the remedies under the Equal Pay Act was lost, since it is of course important to spell out what is likely to happen if the employer does not simply pay up.

Notes

1. [1994] IRLR 460
2. [1998] IRLR 656

SECTION 3

EXAMINATION PRACTICE AND FEEDBACK

4 EXAMINATION QUESTIONS AND FEEDBACK

Section A: the case study

The examination is divided into two sections. Section A is loosely labelled a case study, although to be accurate it is a collection of different scenarios that use the same organisation as a means to tie them together – a common ploy in law examinations for which no apology is made. This section is compulsory and carries 50 per cent of the marks. A minimum of 40 per cent must be scored in this section before a pass mark can be awarded. The same applies to Section B, which is covered later, except that in Section B there is an element of choice.

The key to the case study is in understanding that it always, yes always, covers some aspect of discipline and dismissal. The instructions at the end put you in the position of a personnel practitioner and ask you to give legal advice to a manager who has already acted and/or who is contemplating action in a number, often three, of different situations.

Before we look at recent examination papers here is some general advice on tackling problem questions such as the case study.

Read the question

The CIPD examination gives 10 minutes' reading time, and this should be sufficient to read the paper through slowly at least twice. This gives you time to think about your first impressions – and also to modify them in the light of reflection. It also allows you to start planning your answer in terms of structure. How are the marks allocated? There will be specific advice at the end of the question, which is given in terms of time, for example, 'in answering these questions you should allocate roughly equal amounts of your time to each'.

Clearly the marks follow the time, so you should apportion your time as advised. If it seems that one part is much shorter than the

others despite equal (or longer) allocation of time, it may be that you
have missed something and need to reread the question.

Answer the question

This simple statement will be repeated a number of times throughout this book, but is slightly less relevant for the case study, as the
advice you will give will be similar regardless of who it is that
requires your advice, since the law is the same, for example, whether
you are the one terminating the contract or the one whose contract
is being terminated. Do not get too distracted by the format of the
advice required either. The law has technical language, which needs
to be used and has been explained in an earlier chapter, and legal
sources must be quoted. Normally law examinations will simply
give the instruction 'Advise X', but the CIPD wish to convey an air
of realism and therefore the instruction is couched in terms such as

> Prepare a memo setting out your recommendations and advice,
> drawing as appropriate on case law, relevant published
> research and wider organisational practice. (May 2004)

To reiterate, the memo *must* use the correct legal terms and quote the
relevant legal sources, or several marks will be lost.

It is also important to note that the rubric specifically mentions
'relevant published research'. This does not necessarily mean that
the case study was devised *because* of some recent research (which
may be the case in some other CIPD subjects), merely that you
should draw on relevant wider reading, for instance, if there has
been some discussion as to the authority of case law on a particularly complex issue.

Diagnosis: spotting the issues

One of the reasons problem questions are set is because in reality
this is the context in which legal advice is usually required. The
doctor analogy is a useful one. A patient goes to the GP and
describes certain symptoms. On the basis of these the doctor sifts

through all the possible diagnoses and comes up with the most likely cause(s) of the symptoms. If the matter is relatively simple the doctor will then explain immediately the diagnosis, the treatment and the prognosis. Of course, the analogy breaks down a little because in reality the doctor is likely to ask certain questions and perhaps do certain basic tests to clarify matters. In the case study you need to make a diagnosis on the facts as stated, and will not be able to clarify issues if they are uncertain or unclear. Lawyers will always interview clients to ensure they have all the relevant facts, since in many cases it is not possible to give accurate advice without them. Part of the skill of problem solving is identifying which facts are important, which less so, and which are missing and need to be identified.

As an example, it was once necessary to know how many hours a week an employee worked, because those working between 8 and 15 hours a week were only able to claim unfair dismissal if they had been employed continuously for five years or more. Nowadays a year's service is normally required to claim unfair dismissal, and the number of hours worked per week is irrelevant. In many cases you will be told how long a person has been employed and their status, but if you are not you need to make certain assumptions and state that these are being made. For example:

> It is not stated how long Jane has been working for the organisation or her status. It would appear that she is an employee. If this is the case and she has been employed for at least a year, she may be eligible to claim unfair dismissal as set out in the Employment Rights Act 1996 ...

This is where the 'case study' takes a paradigm shift. In reality, you would either know or be able to check relatively easily whether a person was or was not an employee (or at least view any relevant paperwork and have a rational basis for any assumptions), and of course you would quickly be able to establish length of service.

Please do not fill your script with lots of questions that need answering before giving any advice, but as outlined in the example above, identify the missing facts and make the assumptions accordingly. More guidance on identifying relevant issues is given below.

Stating the law and applying it to the facts

For the PDS Employment Law examination students are permitted to take into the examination a clean copy of employment law statutes and associated regulations. This means it is possible for the examiner to ask more searching questions, and in theory it should give students more confidence in their studies, as there is now no requirement to learn huge chunks of statute. Clearly marks are not going to be awarded for accurately copying out of a book, and you therefore need to learn a short précis of key definitions. Whenever you state the law it must be clear that this is what you are doing. Remember the whole point of the examination is for you to be able to demonstrate that you have learned the law, not that you are coming up with eminently sensible advice that an intelligent individual with a background in human resource management might give. The distinction is the ability to quote the source of the law, either by stating the relevant statute, regulations or the name of the case. Once you have quoted the relevant law it should be applied to the facts in the case as given in the examples below.

Sometimes you will be called upon to make a value judgement. As an example, if a disabled clerical employee with little experience is requesting to move to another job and proposes a move to a senior post with a professional role, you will need to compose an answer setting out the requirements of the Disability Discrimination Act 1995 s6 in relation to reasonable adjustments, and stating that the employer only needs to make such adjustments that are practicable. You should then apply the law to this situation and state that it is unlikely that the proposed move would be deemed to be a reasonable adjustment, since the employee is unlikely to have the necessary skills and that the training time and costs might well not be practicable.

Structure and commentary

Unlike your coursework, which is done in a comparatively leisurely timeframe, examination answers in employment law do not require a formal introduction and conclusion. You might be tempted to summarise the facts of the problem by means of an introduction, but this is just a waste of time and will not earn any marks. Similarly, even though the question may ask for a 'memo' format there is no need (as many candidates did in May 2004) to take this literally as shown below:

> Memo
> To: Stella's manager
> Date: May 2004
> From: Amy Winehouse
> Re: Stella's claim for equal pay

And yes, some candidates really did put their real name on the memo, thus destroying the anonymity guaranteed by the candidate numbering system …

It is also important to quote the law as it currently stands, unless you are asked to make recommendations for the future, which may have to take into account proposed changes in the law. (This was also noted in Chapter 3.)

It is of course important to say what is not covered by the law, so it was acceptable to state, for example, in May 2003, that sexual orientation discrimination was not covered by the Sex Discrimination Act 1975 but was due to become unlawful by means of Regulations to be implemented in December 2003.

One of the distinctive features of 'M'-level answers is the ability to critically evaluate the law. This skill does not usually have to be demonstrated in the case study, since it is essentially practical in nature, although if the facts seem to indicate that organisational policies or procedures need improving, a constructive recommendation may well be appropriate.

Identifying the generic issues

Discipline and dismissal

Let us start with these, since it has already been stated that discipline and dismissal are *always* topics that come into the case study. Sometimes there has been a dismissal, sometimes there is a situation that could lead to a dismissal, or a manager has indicated that he or she would like to dismiss. Discipline is often relevant too, and if so, reference needs to be made to the *ACAS Code of Practice* and the statutory right to be accompanied to disciplinary hearings. Occasionally it will not be clear whether there has been a dismissal, since the employee might have left using ambiguous language, which in turn may lead to a discussion of the law relating to constructive dismissal (as in the May 2003 paper – see below). If there is a proposal to dismiss, the five potentially fair reasons for dismissal can be listed, the most appropriate reason identified, and a brief statement of the requirement to act reasonably in the context of the facts provided. Remedies for a successful unfair dismissal claim should be stated, with current compensation limits. If details of salary, length of service and age are given, you should attempt an estimate of the basic award, for which marks will be awarded. It is the formula for which you score, so do not worry if your maths are inaccurate!

Status

Status is important for many employment rights, and often you will be told the status of the parties in the case study. If this information is omitted but the facts would seem to indicate there might be a dispute as to status, you will need to state how the law would identify the parties' relationship by applying the appropriate tests. Of course, it is important to know why status may be relevant. Discrimination rights, for example, accrue to all workers regardless of whether or not they are employees. Most of the family-friendly rights, however, are only available to employees, as are the rights to claim unfair dismissal and a redundancy payment.

Contractual rights

The case study will occasionally identify specific rights that have been agreed by the parties, but it is more likely that you will need to explain what implied rights exist. If you are not told about notice provisions, for example, you need to explain the statutory minima as set out in ss86 and 87 of the Employment Rights Act 1996. If these have not been adhered to, there is a possibility of a claim for breach of contract, that is, wrongful dismissal. It is also possible that implied rights have been broken: for example, mutual trust and confidence.

Statutory rights

If there has been a dismissal or the threat of one, then as outlined above there must be a discussion of the relevant statutory provisions including eligibility and remedies. There is also a possibility of discrimination aspects being relevant, but this will usually be clearly signposted: for instance, the worker will come from an ethnic minority, or be pregnant, have some impairment, or be the victim (or perpetrator) of harassment. If the law is new (as with Religion or Belief Regulations) it may be important to discuss applicability. An example is the last part of the May 2004 case study. Occasionally there may be health and safety issues involved, which may require a risk assessment or the application of Working Time Regulations. This list could go on and on as there are so many statutory rights and duties, but it should be apparent from a careful reading of the facts which are relevant. (See, for example, Wendy's wish to change her working hours in the last part of the May 2004 case study, which require a discussion of the flexible working provisions as set out in s80F Employment Rights Act 1996 and the two sets of Flexible Working Regulations 2002.)

Other legal rights

Occasionally the law of tort may need to be mentioned because of the duty of care of the employer, which could give rise to an action in negligence if breached. The word 'stress' usually rings the appropriate Pavlovian bells, but do be careful: not all 'stress' has legal implications. It has to be clearly foreseeable to the employer that the employee will become ill because of stress before liability will arise (see, for instance, *Barber* v *Somerset County Council*)[1] but vicarious liability may be relevant if there is personal injury to fellow employees or others.

Good practice and other general guidance

It will sometimes be possible to earn marks for mentioning good practice, but this is *very* rare despite the wording in the examination rubric quoted above asking students to draw on 'wider organisational practice'. Remember that one of the Professional Standards' operational indicators is that practitioners must be able to 'act as the primary adviser to the organisation on employment law'. Many of you will have a great deal of practical knowledge covering workplace issues and how to handle them, but this examination is designed to test your knowledge of the law and not these other aspects. If the law is about to change – for example, the introduction of age discrimination legislation – it may be appropriate to make it clear that although such matters are not currently covered by the law, it would be good practice to handle relevant incidents with sensitivity.

Operational matters should also not be discussed. Disciplinary hearings can sometimes be emotional affairs but the ACAS Code does not address such aspects, and 'sitting employees down', 'ensuring there are plenty of tissues available' and 'providing a glass of water' (all of which have been written about in past law examinations) will not earn marks. If you are not sure what is relevant and what is not, ask yourself, 'Would my organisation be happy to pay a legal adviser large sums of money to have this advice?' If the answer is negative, do not write it down!

Practice papers

Here you will find Section A from the first PDS examination paper, which was set in May 2003, and also that of May 2004. These are used as a basis to analyse the topics covered and suggest approaches to answering the questions. It is very important that you do not think of this guidance as a model answer. To set examination questions on a topic is to provide you with an opportunity to set out the relevant law. Sometimes, but rarely, students write about aspects that the examiner thought were peripheral, but if the case is made for their inclusion and the law is clearly stated, then marks will be given. Although marks are never deducted for errors, if a script is borderline and there are more than a couple of mistakes, it is unlikely that it will be upgraded to a pass.

May 2003 SECTION A – Case Study

(Note: It is permissible to make assumptions by adding to the case study details given below provided the essence of the case study is neither changed nor undermined in any way by what is added.)

David, Emma, Frank and Gerry all work for Allpower, a company providing electricity and gas to customers in northern England.

David, aged 16, has only been with the company six weeks and is finding the transition from college to work extremely stressful. He has already been warned about arriving late for work on three separate occasions.

Emma, aged 23, has been with the company for two years and has a three-year-old daughter.

Frank is 55 and has been with the company for 35 years. He has been an accounts manager for twenty years and has recently been moved, at his request, to another section where the work is slightly less pressurised.

Gerry is the manager responsible for David, Emma and Frank.

You are the Personnel Officer at Allpower. You have been asked to give appropriate advice to Gerry identifying the specific legal issues to be addressed in each of the following cases. Prepare a memo setting out your recommendations and advice.

1. David has been late on two further occasions and has been interviewed by Gerry. It emerged that the main reason David has been late is because of his elderly father, who has recently required help in the mornings. David is the only other person in the household. David has asked if he can be allowed to start work later. Gerry feels that David may prove to be unreliable and wants to dismiss him.

2. Emma, who has always been a conscientious worker, has informed Gerry that she is pregnant and would like to start her maternity leave in September, two months before her baby is due. In the meantime she would like to work from home on one day a week starting next month. Gerry feels that if he gives in to her, everyone else will want the same rights.

3. Frank's performance has deteriorated considerably since his move and there have been two separate complaints that he has been rude to female administrators. Gerry

> called Frank to his office 'for a friendly chat' but ended
> up giving him an oral warning. The exchange was heated
> and resulted in Frank leaving the office saying 'stuff the
> job – I'm not putting up with this any longer'.

*[You should spend 20% of your time on question 1, 40% of your time
on question 2 and 40% on question 3.]*

I. David

A brief word first about the instructions. Although the question
states that a memo should be prepared, the answer should be full
of law and not much else. Do not waste time with preliminary
introductory material, as many candidates did (sometimes using
their real name and organisation as in the example given above) in
the form of a mock memorandum. Start quoting law as soon as
possible.

The question states that David is 16. Is this relevant to the legal
advice that you will be giving? As he is over the minimum school-
leaving age the only applicable law relates to risk assessment and
working time, neither of which would appear to be relevant here.
Thus, his age would appear to be a red herring. It may impact on
whether you to decide to discuss at length the 'stressful' experience
of his transition to work. There is a tendency for all students on
seeing the word 'stress' to write long paragraphs about employer
liability for psychiatric breakdown, although this is extremely rare in
practice. Those who have read the question carefully will note that
Frank, in part 3, is probably more worthy of a discussion about
stress. It is rare for a subject to be deliberately covered in two
separate questions.

There is thus a situation where Gerry, the manager, would like to
dismiss David for being unreliable as he has been late on three occasions in six weeks. There are some mitigating circumstances in that
David has at least some responsibility for his dependent father.
These are the relevant facts, but there are no marks to be gained for
restating them in this format.

The key legal issues are listed below:

- Having been employed for only six weeks David has no employment protection rights in relation to unfair dismissal under the

Employment Rights Act (ERA) 1996. It is assumed that all three (he, Emma and Frank) are employees since there is no indication that they are employed under contracts for services.

- A request to start work later may well be reasonable but there is no legal requirement that it should be considered, let alone granted. The Flexible Working Regulations 2003 only apply to those with 26 weeks' service who have dependent children under the age of 6 (or 18 if disabled).

- Time off to care for dependants (s57A ERA) is available regardless of length of service, but this is unpaid and intended for unforeseen short-term arrangements, and is therefore not appropriate.

- David's proposal to vary his contractual hours of work may be accepted or rejected by his employer, and is governed by general contract law. There is no requirement under the common law for this to be considered or agreed to.

- The terms of David's contract will need to be examined to see if there are any provisions relating to a probationary period. If, as is common, the usual disciplinary procedures do not operate, David has very few rights.

- The statutory right to be accompanied to any meeting that could result in a disciplinary outcome (s10 Employment Relations Act 1999) does not require any length of service and therefore any discipline/dismissal interview must allow David this right. Two weeks' wages by way of compensation are payable if this right is infringed.

- If any disciplinary procedures do apply during probationary periods, then any failure to follow them will amount to breach of contract. Due notice in accordance with the contract must also be given, or payment in lieu if such is provided for. The statutory minimum notice after six weeks' service is one week (s86 ERA).

- Failure to give due notice or other contractual breach may give rise to an action for breach of contract, that is, wrongful dismissal. This is available regardless of length of service, and damages will be awarded to put David in the position he would have been had the contract been performed. He would thus be awarded his wages for the relevant period.

Some students were confused about the operation of flexible working and time off for dependants. It is of course conducive to good employment relations for an employer to consider reasonable requests to change working hours, but there is no legal obligation. A statement such as 'you are required to reasonably consider David's request' is thus inaccurate, or to be more brutal, wrong.

There may be a contractual right to be represented at disciplinary interviews but the statutory right is limited to a companion. It is important to be clear – a statement that David has a right to be represented is wrong.

Be very clear about rights and remedies and how and when they will be available. Vague statements such as 'we will be faced with an employment tribunal' or (worse) 'we could be taken to a tribunal' with no explanation about why will earn no marks.

2. Emma

Every aspect of this question has some relevance and there are no wasted words, except perhaps that she is a 'conscientious worker'. The key legal issues are:

- Emma's service entitles her to both ordinary maternity leave (OML) and additional maternity leave (AML). The Employment Act 2002 amends the Maternity and Parental Leave Regulations 1999 and provides for 26 weeks' OML and another 26 weeks' unpaid AML. She has complied with the statutory notice (only 28 days' notice is required).

- Emma is entitled to statutory maternity pay for six months paid at 90 per cent of her salary for the first six weeks followed by a payment of £100 per week (as at May 2003), or her contractual provisions if greater. There are various conditions that must be complied with if the statutory provisions operate: for instance, production of a medical certificate stating the expected week of childbirth.

- There is insufficient information to discuss the right to return, but her full contractual rights except pay continue during OML, and during AML she is entitled to the benefits of her employer's obligations in relation to trust and confidence.

- As Emma has been employed for 26 weeks and has a child under 6 she can exercise her right to request flexible working under the provisions of the Employment Act 2002 and the Flexible Working Regulations 2003. Various conditions have to be complied with in order to exercise this right: for example, it must be in writing, set out that it is a request to exercise the statutory right of flexible working, confirm that she is the mother of the child, explain what effect, if any, the proposed change will have and how it could be dealt with, and specify the working pattern applied for – in this case to work from home one day a week.

- Gerry has a choice – he can either agree to the change or hold a meeting. He cannot simply reject her request. Agreement to the change or setting up a meeting must be done within 28 days. Emma may bring a companion.

- Serious consideration must be given to the request. Within 14 days of the meeting Emma must be notified of the agreed new pattern and start date or a compromise, or if the request cannot be met, the reason why, and how Emma may appeal.

- It is only possible to reject Emma's request for certain prescribed reasons, and not because Gerry feels 'everyone else will want the same rights'. Prescribed reasons include the burden of additional costs, detrimental effect on ability to meet customer demand or on quality or performance.

- The request, if granted, will become a permanent contractual change unless otherwise agreed, and another request cannot be made within 12 months.

- If the procedure as set out above is not followed, Emma may submit a claim to a tribunal. They may not question the commercial validity of the decision but they can examine the business grounds for refusal. Remedies consist of sending a case back for reconsideration and compensation of up to eight weeks' pay.

- It is highly likely that Emma could submit a claim for sex discrimination under the Sex Discrimination Act (SDA) 1975 alleging either direct discrimination (less favourable treatment) or indirect discrimination (that there is a provision, criterion or practice that is being applied to her that a considerably larger proportion of women than men cannot comply with). She needs to show detriment and the employer must not be able to justify it. If she succeeds in such a claim, remedies comprise a declaration, recommendation and unlimited compensation including an element for injury to feelings.

Students generally recognised the main thrust of the question and wrote well on the key elements of flexible working. Because the 2003 Regulations were only recently published and not in the statute book, marks were awarded for accurate detailed summaries of the rights.

Remedies were less likely to be mentioned, and a few answers moved so seamlessly from a discussion of flexible working to sex discrimination that it was not possible to tell whether the difference was understood.

A few ignored any discussion of the implications of Emma's pregnancy and lost valuable marks by failing to mention any of her rights in relation to maternity leave and pay. The memo format also led some to waste time on empty blurb, such as 'should you require any further guidance please give me a call' or general non-legal remarks: 'Emma is a conscientious worker and it would be a shame to lose her.' Needless to say, none of these earn marks.

3. Frank

The main thrust of this part of the case study is again discipline and dismissal, and the status of Frank's departure. There is very little detail about the rudeness to the administrators, and this should not be discussed in too much depth.

The key legal issues are:

- Frank's eligibility (unlike David) to claim unfair dismissal. If the preliminary requirements for making such a claim under the ERA were not set out in the first section, they should be set out here. The need for dismissal deserves particular attention and is addressed further below.

- Failure to perform comes under the heading of 'capability' and is one of the five potentially fair reasons for dismissal stated in s98 ERA. Conduct – his rudeness to administrators – is also a reason, but in order to dismiss fairly Gerry must act reasonably, which would include following any company disciplinary procedure and complying with the ACAS Code of Practice 1 on disciplinary procedures. With regard to his conduct an investigation would need to be carried out. A 'friendly chat' would be unlikely to be seen as within the Code, but the heated exchange led to disciplinary action in the form of an oral warning, which should have been covered by the Code, and Frank should have been given notice of the meeting and what was to be discussed.

- Frank, as events turned out, was disciplined without the right to be accompanied being offered to him, and therefore the employer is in breach of s10 Employee Relations Act 1999, and Frank will have a right to claim two weeks' pay (s11 of the same Act).

- Frank can only claim unfair dismissal if he can establish that a dismissal as defined by s95 ERA occurred. The only possible ground would be that the employer's actions (via Gerry) amounted to repudiation of contract, and that Gerry was thus entitled to terminate the contract without notice: that is, that Frank has been constructively dismissed. The need for repudiation was stressed by *Western Excavating* v *Sharp*.[2]

- This was a 'heat of the moment' exchange and it is therefore necessary for the employer to ensure that Frank intended to leave his job permanently (*Kwik-Fit* v *Lineham*).[3] It will be up to the tribunal to decide whether Frank's actions amount to a resignation or whether there are grounds for claiming constructive dismissal, although the latter conclusion seems unlikely on the facts.

- If Frank were to be successful in claiming unfair dismissal there are a number of remedies available: reinstatement, re-engagement and compensation. Compensation comprises the basic award, which is calculated according to age, wage and length of service, and the compensatory award. A basic award here would amount to around £7,000 assuming Frank's weekly wage equals or exceeds the (then) statutory limit of £260.

• If Frank does return to work the rudeness to the female administrators requires investigation, as stated above, as it may be that it
  amounts to sexual harassment as in *Reed and Bull* v *Stedman* [4]
  Harassment was not yet defined under UK law when this question was set but the EC Code of Practice was used by the courts. If
  harassment is established, the female administrators may make a
  claim of direct discrimination under the SDA. The burden of proof
  is such that if there appears to be a case to answer, the employer
  will have to provide evidence that there is a non-discriminatory
  reason for the actions (because of the changes made by the 2001
  Regulations).[5] The employer will be deemed vicariously liable for
  Frank's behaviour (*Jones* v *Tower Boot Co Ltd*)[6] unless a defence can
  be established under s41(3) SDA: that is, that steps that were
  reasonably practicable were taken to prevent Frank from acting in
  such a way. The fact that Frank has recently been under pressure
  and moved to this section may be of relevance here.

This aspect of the case study was generally done well, although
sometimes the emphasis was a little skewed in that there was a great
deal of discussion about the general aspects of unfair dismissal, and
very little about the definition of dismissal, and whether Frank
could claim to have been constructively dismissed. Disciplinary
aspects were often not covered in sufficient detail. The issues of
harassment – or possibly bullying – were sometimes ignored
entirely, and some candidates wrote far too much about stress and
the likelihood of Frank claiming hundreds of thousands of pounds,
which seems virtually impossible on the facts as stated.

Remedies for unfair dismissal were usually touched on, although
there is often confusion about how the basic award formula operates: for example, it is assumed that Frank or anyone aged over 41
can claim 1.5 times their weekly wage times the number of years
service regardless of how old he or she is.

May 2004 SECTION A – Case Study

**Note: It is permissible to make assumptions by adding to the
case study details given below provided the essence of the
case study is neither changed nor undermined in any way by
what is added.**

Stella, Ned, Ted and Wendy are all employed by Morasco, a large organisation which sells electrical household goods through a national chain of superstores. They work in the flagship store in South London known to all employees as The Main Shop.

Stella works in the staff canteen and cooks meals for around 250 people each day. She has been employed for 10 years and has recently reduced her hours from 42 a week to 30. She earns £5.50 per hour and has free lunches as part of her terms and conditions.

Ned is a stock controller working in the warehouse. He works full-time and has been employed for eight years.

Ted is a section manager who is in charge of refrigerators. He has only recently transferred to Morasco as Morasco bought out his previous employer, a small high-street chain of shops selling white goods. Ted has found the transfer difficult as the bureaucratic requirements are very complex in his new role and he missed most of his induction due to illness.

Wendy is a checkout operator who came to England from Poland in 1994. She has worked for Morasco for three years and is a popular member of staff. She is a single mother with a young family whose youngest daughter (aged 12) suffers from cerebral palsy.

Assume you are a personnel officer based in the personnel department of The Main Shop. You are requested to give appropriate advice to your managerial colleagues identifying the specific legal issues which should be addressed in each of the following cases. Prepare a memo setting out your recommendations and advice, drawing as appropriate on case law, relevant published research and wider organisational practice.

1. **Stella has learned that she is paid £1 per hour less than her friend Ned. Ned used to earn an even higher wage when he was transferred from the stock control software development office two years ago and took a 10 per cent wage cut since he was suffering from high blood pressure**

and preferred the stress-free environment of the warehouse. Stella has requested that she be paid the same wage as Ned.

2. In the last four months Ted has received two formal warnings for failing to follow procedures when giving refunds. One of these was for failing to give proper instruction to a new member of staff and the other was given when Ted himself was on the service desk because of staff illness. Ted was told his performance must improve dramatically or 'the penalties will be very serious'. He has now 'mislaid' an order from a very rich celebrity who regularly spends a great deal of money in The Main Shop and his manager feels that he should be dismissed. Ted's former disciplinary procedure would normally have allowed him a final written warning before dismissal was contemplated.

3. Wendy has recently become a member of the Polish Liberation Church (PLC), a semi-religious political group which meets regularly to pray, exchange news and lobby Parliament for improvements to education for those of Polish origin. She approaches personnel with two requests (a) that she be allowed to leave work 30 minutes early every Tuesday to go to a PLC meeting, and make up the time on a Wednesday morning and (b) that she no longer be required to work Saturdays as there is a special day school run on Saturdays for those in the area who have cerebral palsy and she will be required to take her daughter there and bring her home.

[*In answering these questions you should allocate roughly equal amounts of time to each.*]

A slightly different approach has been taken here. Rather than going through all the key points, a sample of a good answer has been reproduced and also a marginal fail. These are then discussed.

It is important to remember that these examples are taken verbatim from actual scripts that were of course written under examination conditions.

1. Stella

First, a good answer that earned a merit mark.

> Under the Equal Pay Act 1970, there is a requirement that there is equal treatment for men and women in the same employment and this can include benefits.
>
> From April 2003 an employee can request that under the Equal Pay Act the company conduct an equal pay questionnaire. The employee must choose the comparator and in this case it is Ned.
>
> Under the Equal Pay Act a claim can be brought under:
> (a) like work
> (b) work of equal value
> (c) work rated as equivalent.
> In this case it would be work of equal value.
>
> The employee must put forward the comparator to the Employment Tribunal and an independent official will be appointed to conduct the research and present the findings to the employment tribunal.
>
> The claim if successful can be backdated for up to six years.
>
> The first case in the UK was *Hayward* v *Cammell Laird* [7] where Hayward chose as the comparator a forklift truck driver and was successful.
>
> Factors to be taken into consideration are whether there are other women in the company conducting the same job as Ned and their pay.
>
> The company can raise a defence of genuine material factor due to Ned already taking a deduction in wage due to change of job. The company may have red circled Ned's wage or if it is at the market rate this could be a defence.
>
> If the completion of an analytical job evaluation scheme has taken place, this can also be used in the defence in an equal pay claim.
>
> *Shields* v *E Coomes (Holdings) Ltd* [8]

Note that the answer is quite brief and there are some gaps – which is why it did not score a distinction mark. Some of the omissions:

- The fact that Stella works part-time is irrelevant. The Part-Time

Workers (Prevention of Less Favourable Treatment) Regulations 2000 provides that part-time workers must not be paid less than full-time workers just because they are part-time.

• It is possible that Ned is covered by the Disability Discrimination Act 1995 and that his job and pay are as a result of a 'reasonable adjustment' under s6. If this is the case Stella, who is not disabled, cannot compare herself with Ned.

There is however the correct name of the statute quoted, a clear statement of the three heads under which equal pay is claimable, the choice of the most appropriate (equal value) and an illustrative case. The answer also mentions the employer's defence and gives a likely example of why Ned is being paid more (red circling). The answer also touches on the remedy available and states that back pay may be claimed for up to six years. The use of the equal pay questionnaire is also mentioned.

The mere stating of the name of the case at the end of the answer did not score any marks, as there was no context given.

Here by way of comparison is an answer (from the same centre) that was a weak marginal fail:

Under the Equal Pay Act 1970 (EPA), which is incorporated into the Employment Act 1996, Stella is able to request an equal pay questionnaire.

In this instance the work that is being completed is not like for like as in the case *Shields* v *E Coombes (Holdings) Ltd*[9] where female workers in a betting shop were successful in obtaining an equal pay claim.

Where the work is equivalent then an equal pay questionnaire can be requested. Stella will need to approach her manager and request the information; the employer will not need to disclose any information prior to the tribunal if the matter is not settled prior, in house.

S1 EPA states that where a job has been rated as equivalent using a valid job evaluation scheme then the work will be rated as equal value.

Defence for the employer

Where there is a genuine material difference the employer is justified to dismiss the request for the equal pay claim.

A genuine occupational requirement can consist of the following:
- differences in academic qualifications
- length of service
- method of entering employment
- red circling
- market factors.

Where the employer has acted unreasonably and unjustly with regards to the equal pay claim Stella will be able to take the equal pay claim to the employment tribunal. Here they will either request a reconsideration where no analytical job evaluation has been used or accept the equal pay claim and provide compensation that can be backdated by six years.

The two answers are similar in length but there is no clear statement of the relevant law in the latter (in fact it is quite muddled) and the only case quoted is given as an example of one that does not apply to this particular claim! There is further evidence of confusion (genuine material difference seems to change into a genuine occupational requirement) and although potential defences are listed there is no application of the law to this particular problem, so it would appear the student has no idea which defence (if any) is likely to apply in the case of Stella.

There are always bonus marks awarded for good use of statute and case law (up to 10 per cent of the marks available). The first answer earned three bonus marks for quoting the Equal Pay Act 1970 and the Hayward case. The second answer only scored one bonus mark (for the statute).

Common errors:

- A long introduction setting out the law in an abstract way but not making clear which aspects are relevant to the problem.

- Far too much detail on peripheral aspects, for example a whole page on the use of equal pay questionnaires.

- Lack of precision, for example when discussing remedies it is not enough to state, 'a tribunal may hold that Stella's salary should be increased'.

- Factual errors – some thought that as Stella was not doing like

work she had no claim at all, others that the limit to claiming
back pay in all cases was still only two years. Many thought,
'work rated as equivalent' was exactly the same basis of claim as
'work of equal value'. A few thought that Ned could not be used
as a comparator at all because he was not part-time like Stella.

• Failing to discuss either available defences or remedies or both.

2. Ted

Here is an example of a very good answer that was awarded a
distinction:

> Ted may be able to claim unfair dismissal against Morasco if
> the decision goes ahead to dismiss him. Although Ted has
> only worked for Morasco for a short period of time, under the
> Transfer of Undertakings (Protection of Employment) Regu-
> lations 1981 he may be able to claim continuity of employ-
> ment with his previous employer before the transfer took
> place. This will allow him to claim the one years' service
> qualification requirement for unfair dismissal.
>
> Under s 96 Employment Right Act 1996 (ERA) an employee
> is dismissed if one of the following occurs:
> (i)   dismissal with or without notice
> (ii) end of a fixed term contract
> (iii) employee terminates employment as a result of employer's
>   conduct.
> Plainly, if Ted was dismissed it would fall into the first category.
>
> Once dismissal has been proved it is up to the employer to
> prove that it is for one of the five potentially fair reasons for
> dismissal listed in s98 EA: conduct, capability, redundancy,
> illegality or some other substantial reason.
>
> In this case it would appear that Ted could be fairly
> dismissed on the grounds of lack of capability. Any decision
> must fall 'within the band of reasonable responses' (*Jones* v
> *Iceland Frozen Foods*)[10] and not be perverse (*Rentokil* v [*illegi-
> ble*]).[11] In order to satisfy this requirement it is important that
> Ted was offered training, set specific targets and counselled
> before any final decision to dismiss him is taken.
>
> Under *Polkey* v *A E Dayton Services*[12] it is important that the

disciplinary procedure is strictly followed before any final decision to dismiss is taken. Consequently it may be necessary to give Ted a final warning required by his former disciplinary procedure before dismissing him.

If Morasco dismissed Ted he would have three months in which to present a claim to the tribunal. The maximum compensation that would be awarded is £55,000 and this could include damages for injury to feelings (*Dunnachie* v *Kingston-upon-Hull Council*).[13]

More detailed enquiries about Ted's illness should also be made to be certain that the company is not liable under the Disability Discrimination Act 1995 or negligence for stress.

There is little to fault here. The section on remedies failed to mention reinstatement or re-engagement and the basic award of compensation was also omitted, but apart from that the answer scored well, including a bonus for quoting statute and cases.

By comparison here is a marginal fail answer:

Firstly it needs to be established if the old disciplinary procedure is legally binding or not. Under TUPE (Transfer of Undertakings and Protection of Earnings [*sic*] 1981) an employee transferring takes with them their employment contracts and rights.

If Ted's old contract included the old disciplinary procedure it is legally binding and therefore a final written warning must be considered before dismissal. As it has not been necessary to skip stages with the previous two warnings it would be fair to assume it would not be fair in this case to skip the final warning stage.

It must also be considered why the situations are occurring and Ted's lack of following procedures may be a performance issue seeing as he missed most of his induction. Support must therefore be provided to improve, for example, has the returns policy ever been showed Ted or gone through with him? Training may be undertaken and reasonable time given for Ted to improve. This, I assume, has not happened and therefore dismissal could be deemed unfair because a fair and reasonable procedure has not been adopted.

Bear in mind that Ted's continuous service would have

carried over as part of the transfer. If this adds to over one year Ted could claim unfair dismissal at employment tribunal if he was dismissed. One key thing a tribunal will look at is the reason for dismissal, if it is a fair reason and the procedure adopted in the run up to dismissal. If it is considered incomplete or unfair the dismissal could be deemed as unfair, however if it is a conduct issue in Ted's case it may be fair to jump stages or deal with it more harshly instead of counselling improvement.

As can be seen by comparison with the previous answer, there are large gaps and few clear statements of law. The style gives the impression the student may know the legal reasons for saying what she does, but equally she may not! There is no mention of the Employment Rights Act, TUPE is named wrongly and there are no cases. With hindsight I may have marked this a little generously!

This is of course *the* unfair dismissal question, and the bulk of the marks were for this. Many were able to set out the relevant law clearly and earned a reasonable mark for this part.
Common errors:

- Many candidates failed to spot the TUPE point entirely (and thus lost a third of the marks available for this question).

- Many talked of the future and what the law would be when statutory disciplinary procedures have come into effect – this is not much help when the manager needs advice today!

- Others thought that these changes had already come into effect and that as a result the employer would face a rise in compensation levels if procedures were not adhered to.

- Often a lack of precision in the answers. Examples of vague statements that earned no marks are 'it would be a significant legal risk to dismiss Ted', 'Ted has TUPE transferred' (with no explanation of what 'TUPE' was or the significance of such a transfer) and 'I would suggest that the company should show some compassion.'

- Merely restating the facts and giving operational advice also earns no marks, for example, 'we should look carefully at what we can do to help Ted before giving him further warnings. He missed his induction, is struggling with the bureaucratic nature of our processes and has had no support. We should look at training for him, perhaps a mentor or some help and nor discipline him again at the moment.'

- Out of date compensation limits.

3. Wendy

There were very few really good answers to this part of the question, which comprised effectively two parts. Here is one of the few answers that were awarded a distinction.

(a) Firstly we need to decide whether the Polish Liberation Church falls under the protection of the Employment Equality (Religion or Belief) Regulations 2003.

Wendy could argue that you were treating her less favourably and discriminating against her under s3 of the Regulations if you would allow another employee to rearrange their hours in order to be able to practise their religion.

S2 of the Regulations define what is covered by the term 'religion or belief'. A group of people must share that belief and it must be recognised as a religion. In the S[illegible] case it was held that Sikhs were a religion because they had their own set of beliefs, practices and standards.

The fact that the PLC describe themselves as a semi-religious political group means that they would not be covered under the 2003 Regulations because they would not fall within the definition.

Recommendation

You can refuse to allow her to change her hours in order to attend this PLC meeting because it would not fall within the scope of acts protected by the Regulations.

(b) The request to reduce hours so that there is no work on Saturday would be covered by the Flexible Working (Eligibility, Complaints and Remedies) Regulations 2002 and the amendments to the Employment Rights Act 1996 (ERA) inserted by the Employment Act 2002.

Wendy would qualify because she has been continuously

employed for 26 weeks, is the mother of the child and has the responsibility for the upbringing.

Wendy can only assert her right under s80F ERA if cerebral palsy is identified as a disability (s80F(3)). She can only make one request every 12 months (s80F(4)). She can request a change to the hours she works under s80F(1)(a) and the reason she wants to change her hours falls under s80F(1)(b) because it is for her to care for her daughter.

Wendy would need to put her request in writing under s80F(2) stating how the reduction in hours would affect the business.

Recommendations

You can only refuse Wendy's application if cerebral palsy is not a disability because the child would then be too old to qualify, or on the grounds specified in s80G ERA.

If Wendy makes a complaint to the Employment Tribunal she has to do it within three months (s80H) and she could receive as compensation up to eight weeks' pay (s7 Regulations).

If you do refuse her application you need to inform her in writing.

This was a very solid answer with only a few minor gaps and showed the ability to use the statute book well. It would not be helpful to try to reproduce a marginal fail answer to this question because it is in two parts and normally one of them (the latter) was done reasonably well.

Common errors:

- A clear statement that Religion or Belief Regulations definitely would (or would not) apply without any analysis of the definition of religion or any argument as to why they would or would not apply. Most answers ignored the political aspect entirely. One answer read 'this church is not one immediately recognised. I recommend we investigate this religion before advising her she can't have time off' (nothing like an open mind in such matters …!). Another stated: 'as Tuesday afternoons have no religious significance I would refuse this request'.

- There was confusion over some aspects of the flexible working provisions. Some thought it did not apply to any child over 6 (regardless of the disability); others thought that the remedy for non-compliance was two weeks' pay.

Section B: short answer questions

This part is brief since most of the relevant general guidance has been given in the earlier chapters. The new-style PDS paper gives a choice of 7 out of 10 questions to be answered in an hour. Even with the reading time being taken into account this only allows around eight minutes per answer so it is crucial that every word is focused on the main topic.

Before looking at previous papers here is some general guidance on tackling the questions in Section B.

Read the question

You may recall that this was the first piece of advice given earlier in relation to the case study. Do you recognise clearly what the question is requiring you to do? Make sure that you read all the questions through carefully before finally making your choice.

Answer the question

This is another repetition and is the most important advice in the whole book! It is crucial that everything you write is relevant, and you must not waste valuable time on anything that is peripheral. Plenty of examples are provided below. Planning your answer may seem a luxury given the very short time available for writing, but you need to reflect on the key points that must be made in order to answer the question set. Relevant case names may be jotted down. As the examination rubric states, diagrams, flow-charts or bullet points can be used if they will put across your point clearly, but ensure that if you are using bullet points sufficient explanation is given. If you are called upon to make a judgement, for example, to agree or disagree with a statement with reasons, make sure you do make clear your views. If asked to supply examples from your own organisation, make sure the examples you provide illustrate the necessary legal, as opposed to general personnel, context.

You will never be asked merely to describe (or state) the law in a given area, but as a minimum to explain it. This means providing a suitable context, and implicit in the word 'explain' are questions such as 'why' and 'how'. Again, specific examples are given below.

Structure

For most examination answers, and for all coursework assessments, you will have been told how important it is to structure your work: to say what you are going to say, say it and then say what you have said, with use of summaries, introductions, recommendations and conclusions as appropriate. There will not be time for any of this in an eight-minute answer, but you should try to ensure your opening sentence relates directly to the question and that, if relevant, your concluding sentence enforces any view you have been required to adopt. Use all opportunities to quote the relevant legal sources, and if requested to give case examples do try to quote at least one judicial decision.

'M' level and the thinking performer

At the heart of the PDS Standards is the concept of 'postgraduate-ness' and the thinking performer. This is sometimes more difficult to grasp in the context of employment law, since most personnel practitioners have difficulty in ensuring their current practices are keeping pace with the rapid changes in the law, let alone having the luxury of planning their strategy to deal with changes that may sometimes be years ahead. Sometimes questions will be posed that ask you to assess the impact of future planned changes in the law, and it is in this area that you may be able to draw on articles in, for example, *Industrial Law Journal* or *People Management* to give an insight into what the future may hold. Unlike other areas of the PDS Standards, such as Employee Relations or Employee Reward, it is rare that you will be required to reflect on, for instance, the effectiveness of certain developments or the evolution of some legal topic.

The majority of employment law texts, including the CIPD book *Essentials of employment law* by David Lewis and Malcolm Sergeant, contain explanations of the law in varying amounts of detail, with little contextual commentary or references to research. Remember that there will always be at least two questions in Section B of the paper that will specifically require you to incorporate 'recent research' in your answer. Of course you will not know in advance which topics these will be, so if you wish to have the widest possible choice on the paper you will need to supplement your reading of the textbook. This can be done by reading recent articles in relevant journals. Remember if you make no reference whatsoever to 'research' (which may include contextual information or even recent case decisions) you will not gain a pass mark for that question.

Section B: questions from previous papers

Below are samples of the questions set in the May 2003, November 2003 and May 2004 papers, with commentary on examples from the scripts to illustrate both good and bad practice. As with Section A you should not regard what is contained here as a set of model answers, but as a comprehensive guide to what could be included. Because of lack of space and changes in the law certain questions have been omitted, but those that students appear to have found difficult have been included.

> 1. Your line manager has asked you to explain what is meant by the concept of continuity of employment and indicating why it is important in establishing employee rights. (May 2003)

The subject matter of the question was clearly signposted, but there needed to be a balance between the two component parts of the question. The concept of continuity of employment is a statutory one, and those unfamiliar with the details could check by looking up ss210–219 ERA. A brief summary is required with reference to what will and will not break continuity: for example, maternity leave, sickness absence, cessation of work, absence by custom or other arrangement and industrial action do not break continuity, but weeks during which the employee takes part in industrial action or is working abroad do not count (ss215–216 ERA). Very few answers mentioned the topical situation, given recent wars, of armed forces reservists. While away from work on service continuity is unbroken but the weeks away do not count.

The importance of establishing continuous employment in order to be eligible to claim certain employment rights forms the second part of the answer, and a short list of examples will suffice: for example, 26 weeks' continuous employment in order to claim paternity pay, flexible working or adoption leave, one year's continuous employment to claim parental leave or unfair dismissal in most circumstances, two years' continuous employment over the age of 18 to claim a redundancy payment.

The second part of the answer was usually given more attention, with more detail by most students, while the first part of the answer was often glossed over, sometimes with a bald statement that continuity is 'counting the weeks of employment' and so valuable marks were lost.

This question was extremely popular.

> 2. It has been said that the only area in which the UK has stayed ahead of European Union employment law requirements has been in the area of health and safety. Do you agree? Give examples justifying your answer. (May 2003)

It only became clear that this question was ambiguous when marking commenced, since the statement in the question could be asking generally about UK law 'staying ahead' of European Union (EU) requirements, or only in the field of health and safety law. Your examiner intended the latter, and indeed the majority interpreted it this way, but marks were awarded appropriately for the wider approach.

The main statute on health and safety in the UK is the Health and Safety at Work Act (HASWA) 1974, which was passed as a result of the Robens Committee recommendations. This predated any EU Directives and imposed criminal liability on employers who failed to exercise the duty of care towards employees and non-employees. The establishment of the Health and Safety Commission and Executive and the powers of the enforcing inspectors, including the issuing of improvement and prohibition notices, have resulted in numbers of deaths and personal injuries at work dropping dramatically. Health and safety laws emanating from the EU in the form of Directives have normally been translated speedily into appropriate Regulations, such as the Management of Health and Safety at Work

Regulations 1999 which require employers to make risk assessments in relation to women of childbearing age and young persons.

The only area of health and safety law where the UK was extremely reluctant to adopt EU legislation was in relation to the Working Time Directive, which the UK government refused to implement at first, arguing that it was a health and safety issue. After a case against the EU Commission was lost, the Working Time Regulations finally came into force in October 1998 when they should have been implemented in November 1996, so this is one clear example where the UK was dilatory.

This question was not particularly popular, and many answers were general and did not address directly the question posed. Some answers started with a promising opening sentence such as 'Generally it is true to say that the UK has stayed ahead …' but there was usually not a justification of the statement – merely a long summary of the HASWA.

> 3. Explain what is meant by the phrase 'economic torts' and how unions can ensure that they are not held liable for committing them. (May 2003)

This was probably the most straightforward question on the paper, requiring as it did a simple statement of the components of economic torts and how the 'golden formula' defence contained in s219 Trade Union and Labour Relations (Consolidation) Act (TULRCA) 1992 operates.

There are a number of economic torts. Interference with a contract consists of the defendant (the union) persuading or inducing a third party (the employee) to break or interfere with a contract with the claimant (the employer). The defendant must know of the contract and must have intended to induce the breach or interfere with the contract. The employer must show more than nominal damage, and if the defence of justification is pleaded the employer must rebut it (*Timeplan Education Group Ltd* v *National Union of Teachers*).[14] This tort is closely connected with inducing breach of contract, the one most frequently used as the basis of legal action. Inducing breach of contract simply consists of a union instructing its members to strike (direct inducement) or to apply pressure on another employer, for example, by refusing to supply goods (indirect inducement). The tort of conspiracy consists of a combination of two or more people to do an unlawful act or a lawful act by unlawful means. A strike is of course an unlawful act but may be justified in certain circumstances, as in *Scala Ballroom (Wolverhampton) Ltd* v *Ratcliffe*,[15] where the Musicians Union boycott was used to protest against a colour bar at a dance hall. Intimidation is rarely pleaded, but a threat to commit an unlawful act such as breach of contract is actionable (*Rookes* v *Barnard*).[16]

The statutory defence contained in s219 TULRCA has been successfully pleaded in a number of cases, but case law more frequently indicates the limits of the defence as in *Bent's Brewery Co Ltd* v *Luke Hogan*,[17] where it was held there was no imminent dispute so the protection was lost. In *BBC* v *Hearn*[18] the defence also failed since the dispute was held to be mainly political rather than a trade dispute.

This area of law tends not to be popular with students as it is perceived as difficult, so it was hoped this question might encourage a few to tackle a relatively simple aspect. It was not a successful ploy!

> 4. Construct a flowchart for a staff training day drawing on judicial decisions which addresses the main issues raised in deciding whether a merger is going to be subject to the provisions of the Transfer of Undertakings (Protection of Employment) Regulations 1981. (May 2003)

This was another focused question that required an understanding of certain key cases, such as *Spijkers* v *Gebroeders Benedik Abattoir CV*[19] and *Sophie Redmond Stichting* v *Bartol and others*.[20]

A sample flowchart is reproduced opposite, but this is given simply as an indication of the key aspects that could be included.

No case detail is given in the flowchart, but answers may well include a brief summary of key points. The citing of relevant cases at certain points in itself demonstrates an understanding of them.

Some answers did not produce a flowchart as required. This was not itself a reason for failing if all the information was there, but your examiner is constantly requested by CIPD to make the examination more user-friendly and work-related, and it was supposed to

Table 1 Sample flowchart illustrating application of TUPE
Regulations

1. Has there been a sale of assets only?

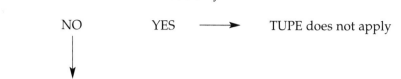

       NO   YES ⟶ TUPE does not apply

2. Is there a stable and discrete economic entity?

       YES   NO ⟶ TUPE does not apply

3. Has this entity been transferred? See Spijkers case[i]

       YES   NO ⟶ TUPE does not apply

4. Has there been a significant transfer of assets or major part of the
workforce?

       YES   NO ⟶ TUPE MAY not apply
                                   Suzen cf[ii]
                                 ECM v Cox[iii]

5. Has there been a transfer of staff but no transfer of tangible assets?

       NO   YES ⟶ TUPE MAY not apply
                                   Oy Liikenne[iv]

       TUPE probably does apply

[i] [1986] ECR 1119.
[ii] [1997] IRLR 255.
[iii] [1999] IRLR 559.
[iv] [2001] IRLR 171.

encourage creative thought. It clearly did not. This was not a very popular question.

> 5. How far is it true to say that an employer has complete freedom in deciding how many and which hours any employee should work? Give appropriate examples from your own organisation. (May 2003)

The starting point for this answer is the contents of the contract that has been agreed between the parties. The more flexible the terms in the contract, the more potential freedom the employer has. It is generally up to the employer to decide how work should be allocated between different employees and to agree, for instance, shift times, time off to compensate for unsocial hours worked and so on. Any proposed variation will be governed by normal contract rules, and so there will normally need to be mutual agreement if hours are to be changed, since imposition of a change may well amount to breach of contract, which could lead to a claim of constructive dismissal.

There are also several legislative provisions that regulate working time, the most important being the Working Time Regulations 1998, which normally limits working hours to 48 per week and makes detailed provisions for rest periods, days off, night shift working, young persons' working hours and so on. Young people are governed by the Management of Health and Safety at Work Regulations (MHSWR) 1999, and children below the minimum school leaving age by the Children (Protection at Work) Regulations 1998. Sunday working is governed by ss36-43 ERA in relation to shop and licensed betting shop workers, but the restrictions apply generally to those employed prior to the relevant law being implemented in August 1994. The recently implemented right to request flexible working will also impact on the employer's freedom, as may the need to make reasonable adjustments for disabled people under the Disability Discrimination Act 1995 or pregnant women on health grounds (MHSWR). It is possible that part-time workers and fixed-term employees may allege that they have been less favourably treated than their full-time or permanent comparators under the Part-Time Workers (Prevention of Less Favourable Treatment) Regulations 2000 and Fixed-Term Employees (Prevention of Less Favourable Treatment) Regulations 2002 if their hours of work are not objectively justified.

The answer should be well rounded and contain both common law and statutory provisions: some contained only the latter. The invitation at the end of the question to give examples must be read in the context of the law, so long lists of, for example, flexitime arrangements with no explanation of why or how the law required or affected their adoption, would not be worthy of marks. Some answers only discussed the Working Time Regulations, and there was a tendency for some to copy out large chunks from the statute book. This also earned no marks. Overall this was a popular question and generally done reasonably well.

6. How has the employer's freedom to monitor employee activities at work been limited by UK law? (May 2003)

The law on monitoring of employee activities has been developing and changing a great deal, and is often dealt with in the textbooks under the right to privacy. The Human Rights Act 1998 incorporates the provisions of the European Convention for the Protection of Human Rights and Fundamental Freedoms into UK law, but it only applies to public authorities. The leading case based on the Convention is *Halford* v *UK*,[21] where, before there was any UK legislation relating to the tapping of phone calls, the act of so doing by the employer was held to be a breach of Article 8, which provides the right to privacy, since the employer had not informed Halford that it was being done. Article 8 provides a defence of justification on the grounds of national security, public safety or to prevent disorder or crime, and on this basis employers may be able to justify the use of CCTV as long as it is not used indiscriminately. Similarly, monitoring of e-mails and Internet use may be protected on the basis that the employer has the right to check employees are not wasting time, or working for a competitor, or accessing websites in breach of company policy. Proportionality is the most important aspect to be taken into consideration.

The Regulation of Investigatory Powers Act 2001 makes interception of a communication in the course of post or telephone or computer a criminal offence if not made with lawful authority. Such interception may however be made lawful if consent is given. There may be some conflict between the provisions of this legislation and that of the Data Protection Act 1998, which imposes restrictions on data processing. Generally such monitoring should only take place if it is established that there is a real need for it and the methods used are realistic. Again, proportionality is important. In addition, the Telecommunications (Lawful Business Practice) (Interception of Communications) Regulations 2000 allow employers to legitimately monitor or record all telecommunications transmitted over their systems without consent for a number of purposes, which include quality control and to ensure compliance with regulatory practices, for example an employer's code on legitimate computer use. There is also a comprehensive Code of Practice on this aspect produced by the Information Commissioner.

As mentioned above, some textbooks cover these matters in some detail, others hardly at all. Students were clearly well informed, and this was reflected in their answers, which tended to be comprehensive. A few weak answers concentrated too much on the Data Protection Act but these were comparatively rare.

> 7. In what circumstances is an employee more likely to claim wrongful dismissal as opposed to constructive dismissal? Explain the financial implications. (May 2003)

This question required students to demonstrate understanding of the basic difference between the contractual and statutory approaches to dismissal, and thus to set out the nature of the common law action for wrongful dismissal in breach of contract and compare it with the statutory concept of constructive dismissal (although good answers should point out that this phrase is not used in the statutory provisions). Since in most cases employees' contracts can lawfully be terminated under contract by the giving of notice, in most cases an unjustified summary dismissal will only result in damages equivalent to the wages payable during the notice period. If an employee does not have the requisite one year's service to claim unfair dismissal this will be the only action open to him or her. In certain cases, for example highly paid entertainers on fixed-term contracts, there may be advantages in bringing such a claim since there is no limit to damages claimed in the High Court. Damages are based on the contract provisions and may be quite high if stock options are involved. In practice most cases of wrongful dismissal are processed by the employment tribunal, which has a limit of £25,000.

Discussion of the concept of constructive dismissal must refer to the need for repudiatory conduct on the part of the employer, as held in *Western Excavating* v *Sharp*.[22] If such conduct has not occurred, an employee will simply be treated as having resigned and no claim will be upheld. If constructive dismissal is unfair – that is, the employer has not acted reasonably – the remedies available consist of reinstatement, re-engagement or compensation. In financial terms the award of compensation may exceed that for wrongful dismissal, but much will depend on the circumstances. The award consists of a basic award, which is calculated according to age, weekly pay and length of service and has a maximum currently of £8,100.[23] In addition; a compensatory award may be made, which will cover loss of earnings past and future and other lost benefits, with a maximum award currently of £55,000.[24] Any compensation awarded may be reduced if there is contribution to the dismissal by the acts of the employee, and the employee must mitigate his or her loss, for example, by actively seeking employment while waiting for the case to be heard.

This was a popular question, which was generally done extremely well, although some were clearly confused about the terminology and so talked of damages and injury to feelings in relation to constructive dismissal, or thought that wrongful dismissal was just another aspect of unfair dismissal.

> 8. Explain the circumstances in which an employee who is made redundant may claim to have been unfairly dismissed. (May 2003)

This is another question that allows students to demonstrate their knowledge of the unfair dismissal legislation and case law. Given that unfair dismissal is the most popular claim at tribunals, your examiner makes no apology for setting yet another question on this area of the law. There are a number of possible reasons for claiming unfair dismissal after having been dismissed by reason of redundancy. They include:

- Redundancy was not the real reason for dismissal because there was not a redundancy as defined by s139 ERA. Cases such as *Safeway Stores plc* v *Burrell*[25] illustrate the employee's attempt to show the dismissal was therefore unfair simply because the reason given was not true.

- The employer has not acted reasonably in treating the redundancy as a ground for dismissal. The leading case is *Williams* v *Compair Maxam Ltd*,[26] which gave guidance on practice that should be adopted, and which has since been adapted to include giving warnings, consultation with unions and individuals, objective agreed selection criteria and consideration of alternative employment. If there is a redundancy selection procedure, this should be followed and any appeal procedure also adhered to.

- If selection is based on any of the reasons specified in ss99–105 ERA, dismissal would be automatically unfair. These include pregnancy or exercise of any rights connected with family such as parental leave or flexible working, dismissal of health and safety representatives, and compliance with Working Time Regulations. Similarly selection for redundancy just because of trade union membership or non-membership would be an unfair dismissal (s152 TULRCA).

- If a redundancy occurs as a result of merger or takeover to which the TUPE Regulations apply it may be an unfair dismissal if the defence of economic technical or organisational reason cannot be upheld (Regulation 8(2)).

There is thus plenty of material available – and the above list is not intended to be exhaustive. Some answers concentrated solely on the forbidden statutory grounds, and given that the statute book was to hand, did not earn many marks for merely reproducing at length extracts from ss99–104 inclusive. Failure to pay a redundancy payment was quoted by some as a reason to claim unfair dismissal, as was being refused time off to look for alternative work. It may be that because this was the last question some trawled through the statute book guessing at possible grounds for claims. The question was popular, although the quality of the answers was very varied.

> 9. To what extent is it true to say that casual, part-time and fixed-term contract workers have the same rights as those with permanent contracts? Justify your answer. (November 2003)

This question addresses the status of different workers and their rights, and requires a legal explanation of the various terms within it. There is a great deal written about atypical workers in most employment textbooks, and this should have been an easy question. It was very popular and was generally done well, but there were comparatively few answers that contained case examples. The most famous case on casual workers is probably *Carmichael* v *National Power plc*,[27] and this could be usefully included in the answer.

Better answers also made reference to Part-Time Workers (Prevention of Less Favourable Treatment) Regulations and Fixed-Term Employees (Prevention of Less Favourable Treatment) Regulations.

> 10. You are asked to give a brief presentation to senior managers on the implications of the new discrimination law coming into effect in 2003. Summarise your main points emphasising actions that need to be taken. (November 2003)

This was another popular question that was generally done reasonably well. The key word here was 'implications', and weaker answers merely described the provisions of the new Sexual Orientation and Religion or Belief Regulations. To obtain a solid pass mark it was necessary to explain the steps necessary to ensure compliance with the new law: for example, check policies on time off for religious festivals, dress codes, food available in staff canteens, promotion criteria and so on.

There was sometimes confusion between the terms 'sexual orientation' and 'gender reassignment' or at least some answers seemed to indicate that the law on gender reassignment discrimination did not come into effect until December 2003 (it was incorporated into the Sex Discrimination Act 1975 in 1999).

> 11. Explain what is meant by vicarious liability and outline the differences (if any) taken by the courts in relation to (a) discrimination cases and (b) liability for negligence resulting in physical injury. (November 2003)

This was a popular question but the pass rate was not good. It would seem that many were unable to think outside the box: that is, students were able to write about discrimination and then about vicarious liability in that context and (occasionally) negligence and vicarious liability in that context, but rarely both. For many it would seem that the concept of vicarious liability was a subset of other topics, and it had never occurred to them to compare the approaches at all.

That said, there were a few solid answers including the following which earned a distinction:

> Vicarious liability is where an employer is liable for the actions of his/her employees when they are done 'in the course of employment'. The concept is associated with two main areas: discrimination and negligence.
>
> In discrimination cases, vicarious liability has been interpreted more widely than in negligence. As *Jones* v *Tower Boot*[28] has shown, 'in the course of employment' can include harassment both in and outside the workplace. In this case it was argued that the term should be approached as a 'layman' would perceive it. *Burton and Rhule* v *De Vere Hotels*[29] famously shows the extent to which vicarious liability can be applied. The applicants claimed under both the Sex Discrimination Act 1975 and the Race Relations Act 1976 and succeeded as it was argued that the employer should have understood the risk associated with asking them to work at a venue where Bernard Manning was a speaker.
>
> In general vicarious liability in negligence has been interpreted in less broad terms. 'In the course of employment' has been taken to mean that an employer will only be found negligent if the action is part of the employee's work. A case in point is *ICI* v *Shatwell*,[30] where the employer successfully used the defence *'volenti non fit injuria'* (the employee had consented to the risk), but this case is now showing its age since more recent cases eg *Lister* v *Hesley Hall Ltd*[31] have widened the meaning of 'in the course of employment'. In this case where an employee's actions are 'closely and directly connected to the work done' the employer is treated as being vicariously liable.
>
> 12. Explain the necessary steps to be taken if an employer wishes to vary a significant term of an employee's contract and the implications if these are not followed. (November 2003)

This was a question that required an understanding of basic legal contractual principles. Unfortunately some took an operational approach and virtually ignored the law, for example, talking about the need for consultation and then imposing the changes regardless of the legal consequences. It was quite a popular question but only a few of those who attempted it obtained a pass grade. Here is one of the better answers that earned a merit grade:

> Variation of a term in an employee's contract is similar to that of forming the original contract of employment. For the term to have legal effect there must be:
> – Offer
> – Acceptance
> – Consideration
> – Intention to create legal relations.
> The employer should provide a written statement containing details of any agreed changes under s4 ERA 1996, not later than one month after the change.
>   Case law is useful in adding to statute in these situations. It shows that employers can include some terms in contracts that mean this procedure need not be followed. These include:
> – Use of wide terms
> – Narrow terms that are 'discretionary' (*Johnstone* v *Bloomsbury HA*)[32] – however the courts have warned against this use of discretionary terms
> – Clauses to change the term with notice.
> However in terms of following the procedure outlined in ERA 1996, case law shows that the issue of offer/acceptance/consideration is important. *Aparou* v *Iceland Frozen Foods*[33] shows that even where an employee appears to have accepted a change by continuing to work, this is not necessarily the case. *Ford* v *Warwickshire County Council*[34] also demonstrates this and reveals that an employee may continue to work and seek a remedy at the same time.
>   The remedy in question may be constructive dismissal (unfair dismissal). The imposed term may be seen as a breach of trust if it is imposed in an unreasonable manner.

13. Your manager has heard that the Employment Act 2002 has implications for the content and operation of disciplinary and grievance procedures. Drawing on recent research, explain what these are and their particular importance to small businesses. (May 2004)

This question was one of the two in the May 2004 paper requiring students to demonstrate wider reading by the use of the phrase 'drawing on recent research'. Those who simply described the new statutory procedures but gave no contextual information at all did not receive a pass mark. This point has been emphasised very clearly in the examiner's report which all students should read, but it is so important that it will be repeated: if no wider reading is demonstrated the answer will fail. 'Research' has been interpreted generously to mean any relevant wider reading including recent case law, ACAS reports (particularly relevant here) or government consultation papers.

The pass rate on this question was the third lowest for the whole paper (the other 'research' question – question 16 below – had the second lowest pass rate). Given that students had the relevant statutory provisions with them in the examination, it should have been apparent that a pass mark could not be earned merely by giving a précis of the relevant law (to be found in the Employment Act 2002 Schedule 2). The question asks for the particular significance of this law for small businesses, and good answers explained (drawing on ACAS research) that small businesses were most likely to be involved in unfair dismissal claims and that this was largely because of a failure to follow any procedures. Small businesses rarely have any formal grievance procedures either, and may therefore be subject to constructive dismissal claims without being aware of the alleged cause of the failure of the employer–employee relationship.

Here is an example of a solid pass answer:

The Employment Act 2002 requires that in October 2004 all organisations are required to have disciplinary and grievance procedures in place. Before the Employment Act 2002, organisations with 20 or less employees were not required to have any procedures in place. In October, all organisations, regardless of size, will need to have a procedure or follow the statutory procedures outlined in s30(1) Employment Act 2002. Details can be found in the schedules to the Act.

Recent research has shown that some organisations do not follow ACAS guidelines on disciplinary procedures and so by making it compulsory the law will increase employees' rights and ensure they are treated fairly and have the chance to speak to the employer before dismissal. In *Robertson* v *Preston CC*[35] a man who wielded an axe in a company restaurant was deemed unfairly dismissed when he was dismissed without a hearing.

14. You have been asked by your manager to provide a brief summary of the relevant law regarding holiday pay and its application to self-employed and casual workers. Explain clearly the main points indicating the most recent developments. (May 2004)

The problem with real employment law issues is that they do not come in compartmentalised boxes with labels attached. Many students know a great deal about holidays and the Working Time Regulations 1998 (WTR). Many also know about pay, from both the contractual and statutory perspective. Not many students knew about 'holiday pay' however – which is what this answer requires. Many wrote a whole page about the WTR and then a sentence at the end along the lines of 'and all holiday should be paid'. Such answers did not pass. The best answers talked of the problems of holiday pay in relation to casual workers (which the question specifically mentioned) and demonstrated their understanding of the latest case law in relation to 'rolled-up' holiday pay, giving examples such as *Marshalls Clay Products* v *Caulfield.* [36]

15. Explain how the statutory approach to terminating employment contracts as a result of long-term sickness differs from the common law approach, assuming that the Disability Discrimination Act 1995 is not relevant. (May 2004)

Another question which required students to distinguish between the common law and statutory approaches – in this case in relation to contract termination. This answer produced the highest fail rate – only 20 per cent of those attempting it passed. Many knew a great deal about the statutory procedures for dismissing for incapability under the Employment Rights Act 1996 and were able to score well for this part of the answer, but knew virtually nothing about common law termination except that normally notice must be given. Understandably, in the circumstances, they found it difficult to write much on how the two approaches 'differed' which was the essence of the answer.

Very few mentioned the concept of 'frustration', which must be discussed. Many thought that an employee being ill amounted to breach, and this enabled the employer to terminate the contract. A frustrated contract is deemed to have been terminated by operation of law, meaning that no breach has occurred and neither party can be liable to compensate the other. Better answers made it clear that courts were reluctant to find contracts had been frustrated as this means that there is deemed to be no dismissal. *Egg Stores* v *Leibovici*[37] is an example of a frustrated contract where the judge clearly set out the considerations for finding that frustration has occurred. In practical terms employers need to err on the side of caution, and in practice will treat long-term sickness as a matter for consultation after having received informed medical advice about the prognosis. It is thus likely that from the employer's perspective the approaches are not dissimilar.

There were some really bad answers which indicated that some students did not understand the phrase 'common law' for example, 'termination by common law can be either by the employer (s95(1)(a)ERA) or by the employee (s95 (1) (c) ERA)'.

16. You have been asked to organise a debate at your local CIPD branch meeting where the proposal is 'This house firmly believes there is no such thing as a right to strike'. Do you consider that this would be a good motion for debate? Drawing on recent research explain why/why not? (May 2004)

This was the other 'research' question but it would appear that students answered it because they saw the word 'strike' and thought it would give them the opportunity to write a great deal about industrial action in general and balloting provisions in particular. The kindest assumption (given that students have a choice) is that having learned a great deal about collective labour law and only finding this one opportunity to demonstrate hours of learning, they internally manipulate the question to mean what they want it to mean – usually 'write all you know about strikes'.

There were very few good answers – some thought there was a legal right to strike (there is not – only immunity from civil liability in certain circumstances) but the few who did achieve a pass drew on practical examples to underpin their argument, for example the recent firefighters' dispute. This was treated as 'research' for the purposes of the question.

It is important to state again that the approaches outlined in this and the previous chapters are only intended as guidelines and should not be treated as comprehensive model answers. Over the years students have come up with perfectly relevant aspects to questions that were never thought of when the examination was set, and your examiner is, despite popular belief, a human being who is prone to human error. If a clear understanding of the topic is demonstrated, the answer will earn a pass subject to the usual caveat that it is necessary to answer the question that has been set.

Notes

1. [2004] IRLR 475.
2. [1978] IRLR 27.
3. [1992] IRLR 156.
4. [1999] IRLR 299.
5. Sex Discrimination (Indirect Discrimination and Burden of Proof) Regulations 2001.
6. [1997] IRLR 168.
7. [1988] IRLR 257.
8. [1978] ICR 1159.
9. As above.
10. [1982] IRLR 439.
11. Unable to trace any case with this as a reason for the decision involving Rentokil – but of course it may be unreported.
12. [1987] IRLR 13.
13. [2004] IRLR 287.
14. [1997] IRLR 457.
15. [1958] 3 All ER 220.
16. [1964] AC 1129 HL.

17. [1945] 2 All ER 570.
18. [1977] IRLR 273.
19. [1986] ECR 1119.
20. [1992] IRLR 366.
21. [1997] IRLR 471.
22. [1978] IRLR 27.
23. Updated – as at April 2004.
24. Ditto.
25. [1997] IRLR 200.
26. [1982] IRLR 83.
27. [2000] IRLR 43.
28. [1997] IRLR 168.
29. [1996] IRLR 596, but note that since this examination this case has been held to have been wrongly decided by the House of Lords in *Macdonald and Pearce* [2003] IRLR 512.
30. [1965] AC 656.
31. [2001] 2 All ER 769.
32. [1991] ICR 269.
33. [1996] IRLR 119.
34. [1983] IRLR 126.
35. Unable to locate this – presume unreported.
36. [2003] IRLR 552.
37. [1976] IRLR 376.

SECTION 4

CONCLUSION

5 CONCLUSION

I have attempted in this second edition to address the comments made by tutors and students in relation to the first edition. There are more examples from student scripts of good answers, and sometimes a few 'marginal' answers for comparison. I have not included a long list of 'essential' cases – key cases are common to most textbooks and students will tend to remember the ones the tutors stress as being important. My views on which cases are essential will no doubt differ from others, and I do not wish to enter into a debate!

The four most important tips for passing the employment law examination are:

1. State the relevant law clearly citing statutes and case names correctly.

2. Where appropriate (for example, Section A) apply the law to the situation.

3. Always state the basis of any legal liability (see 1), any defences available and remedies that will be available if the applicant is successful.

4. *Answer the question set.*

INDEX

A

ACAS *see* Advisory Conciliatory and Arbitration Service
ACAS Code of Practice, 38, 40, 47
Advisory Conciliatory and Arbitration Service (ACAS), 6, 20, 74–5
age discrimination legislation, 40
age regulations, 42, 63
armed forces reservists, 61

B

BACKUP framework, 29
Barnett, Daniel, 20
bullet points, 26

C

CAC *see* Central Arbitration Committee
capability, 46
case studies, 33–59 *passim*
cases, viii–ix, 22–4, 27
Central Arbitration Committee (CAC), 5, 6, 20
Children (Protection at Work) Regulations, 66
children, dependant, 43, 45, 58–9
citation, 21–4, 27
collective bargaining, 13
Commission for Racial Equality (CRE), 6
compensation, 43, 46–7, 53, 57, 68–9
continuity of employment, 61–2
contracts of employment, 10–11, 72–3, 75–6
Court of Human Rights, 6
CRE *see* Commission for Racial Equality

D

Data Protection Act, 8, 67–8
DDA *see* Disability Discrimination Act
disability, 11, 59, 66
Disability Discrimination Act (DDA), 30, 36, 52, 55, 66, 75
disciplinary procedure, 37–8, 40, 43–4, 46–7, 55
discrimination, 11–12, 39, 40, 45–8, 71–2
dismissal, 35, 37–8, 39, 43, 46–8, 54–7, 68–70, 73
dyslexic students, 27

E

Employment Act, 19, 44, 45, 52, 57, 74–5
employment law, 3–13 *passim*, 18–19, 21, 22, 29, 39
Employment Law examination, x, 9, 17, 25, 26–7, 36, 59
Employment Relations Act, 7, 43, 47
Employment Rights Act (ERA), 10, 21, 35, 38, 39, 43, 46–7, 57–8, 61, 66, 69, 70, 73, 76
equal pay, 7, 51–4 *passim*
Equal Pay Act, 30, 51–3
equal pay questionnaire, 51–2
ERA *see* Employment Rights Act
Essentials of Employment Law, 5, 60
EU legislation *see* European Union legislation
European Court of Justice, 6
European Union legislation (EU), 3, 4, 62–3
examination papers, PDS *see*

Section A and Section B
   examination papers
examination techniques, 24–5,
   59–61
examiners' reports, 26, 27–30 *passim*

F
Fixed-Term Employees (Prevention
   of Less Favourable Treatment)
   Regulations, 66, 71
flexible working, 44, 45, 58, 62, 66
Flexible Working Regulations, 39,
   43, 45, 57
flowcharts, 64–5
footnotes, 23

G
golden formula, 13, 63
grammar, 27

H
harassment, 7, 48
HASWA *see* Health and Safety at
   Work Act
health and safety, 13, 62–3
Health and Safety at Work Act
   (HASWA), 13, 62–3
Health and Safety Commission
   (HSC), 6, 62
holiday pay, 75
hours, working, 35, 43, 66
HSC *see* Health and Safety
   Commission
Human Rights Act, 67

I
IDS Brief, 20
industrial action, 13, 61, 64, 76
Industrial Law Journal, 20, 60
Information Commissioner, 68
intellectual property, 8

L
legibility, 27

liability, 72

M
Management of Health and Safety
   at Work Regulations (MHSWR),
   62–3, 66
marks, awarding, 24, 40, 53, 62
Master's-level thinking, 29, 37, 60–1
Maternity and Parental Leave
   Regulations, 44
maternity leave *see* rights,
   maternity
maternity pay *see* rights, maternity
meetings, 45
memos, 34, 37, 41–2, 49
MHSWR *see* Management of Health
   and Safety at Work Regulations
mind mapping, 18–19, 25
M-level *see* Master's-level thinking
monitoring, 67–8

N
negligence, 28, 71–2
'non-employees', 10, 70–1
notice, 43

O
oral warnings, 47

P
Part-Time Workers (Prevention of
   Less Favourable Treatment)
   Regulations, 51–2, 66, 71
PDS *see* Standards, Professional
   Development
People Management , 19, 20, 60
personnel professionals, 3, 22
Personnel Today, 20
'post-graduateness' *see* Master's-
   level thinking
practice examination papers, 40–59
   passim
presentation, 26–7
probationary period, 43

Professional Development Standards (PDS) *see* Standards, Professional Development

R
Race Relations Act, 72
red circling, 51–2
redundancy, 69–70
references, 11, 28–9
Regulation of Investigatory Powers Act, 67
Religion or Belief and Sexual Orientation Regulations, 30, 39, 57–8, 71
research, 21, 29, 34, 76
revision, 17–18, 21, 24–5
rights
    contractual, 38
    employment, 12, 42, 61, 72–3, 75
    human, 7, 67
    legal, 39
    maternity, 7, 12, 44–5, 61
    parental, 7, 12, 62
    paternity, 12, 62
    statutory, 39, 43
Robens Committee, 62

S
scripts, examination, 23, 26–7, 35, 40, 50
SDA *see* Sex Discrimination Act
Section A examination paper, 29, 30, 33–59 *passim*, 61, 81
Section B examination paper, 21, 27, 28, 29, 59–77 *passim*
service, length of, 43
Sex Discrimination Act (SDA), 22, 37, 45, 48, 71, 72
Sexual Orientation Regulations *see* Religion or Belief and Sexual Orientation Regulations
sickness, 75–6
small businesses, 29–30, 74

spelling, 26
Standards, Professional Development (PDS), x, 3, 4–9 *passim*, 21, 29, 39, 60
status, 38
stress, 39, 42
strikes, 64, 76–7

T
Telecommunications (Lawful Business Practice) (Interception of Communications) Regulations, 68
termination of employment, 12–13
textbooks, 19, 36, 60–1
time off, 7, 43
torts, 13, 63
Trade Union and Labour Relations (Consolidation) Act (TULRCA), 63–4, 70
trade unions, 8, 13, 63–4, 70
Transfer of Undertakings (Protection of Employment) Regulations (TUPE), 7, 54–6, 64–5, 70
tribunals, 3, 4, 9 , 44, 45, 51, 53, 55, 58, 69
TULRCA *see* Trade Union and Labour Relations (Consolidation) Act
TUPE *see* Transfer of Undertakings (Protection of Employment) Regulations

W
whistleblowing, 7, 13
workers
    agency, 10, 22
    casual, 10, 70–1, 75
    fixed-term contract, 10, 70–1
    part-time, 10, 51–2, 70–1
    self-employed, 75
    temporary, 10
working relationships, 10
Working Time Regulations (WTR), 39, 63, 66–7, 70, 75